중학 문법+쓰기

클리어.

Level 2

문법 영작과 서술형을 한번에 끝내는
중학 문법+쓰기 클리어

- 영어 문법과 쓰기를 동시에 CLEAR!
- 영작 집중 훈련으로 쓰기 실력 강화 CLEAR!
- 실전 유형으로 서술형 완벽 대비 CLEAR!

학습자의 마음을 읽는 동아영어콘텐츠연구팀

동아영어콘텐츠연구팀은 동아출판의 영어 개발 연구원, 현장 선생님, 그리고 전문 원고 집필자들이
공동연구를 통해 최적의 콘텐츠를 개발하는 연구조직입니다.

원고 개발에 참여하신 분들

강남숙   안태윤   차호윤   홍석현

중학 문법+쓰기

클리어.

Level 2

구성과 특징

영작 기본 훈련 단계 | 문법을 쓰기로 연결하는 체계적인 연습을 할 수 있습니다.
기본적인 형태 연습에서 완전한 문장 쓰기까지의 과정을 통해 영작 실력을 쌓을 수 있습니다.

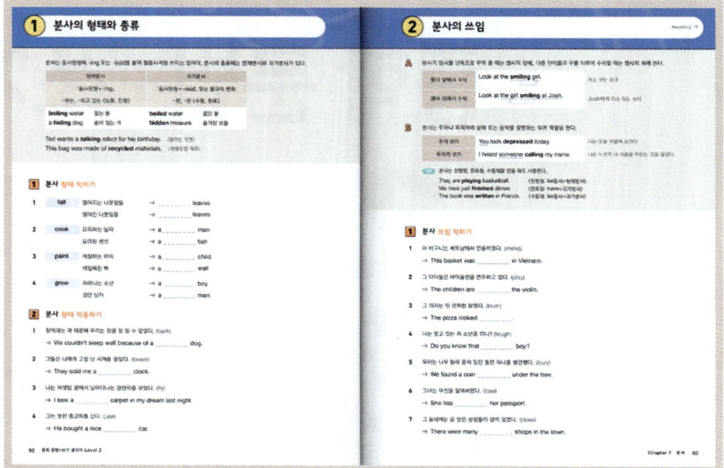

문법 설명 + 기본 형태 학습

세분화된 문법 요목으로 문법 개념을 더 쉽게 이해하고, 기본 형태 학습으로 바로 연습하여 더 쉽게 쓸 수 있습니다.

문장을 쓰기 위한 문법을 학습한 후

바로 해보는 기본 형태 학습

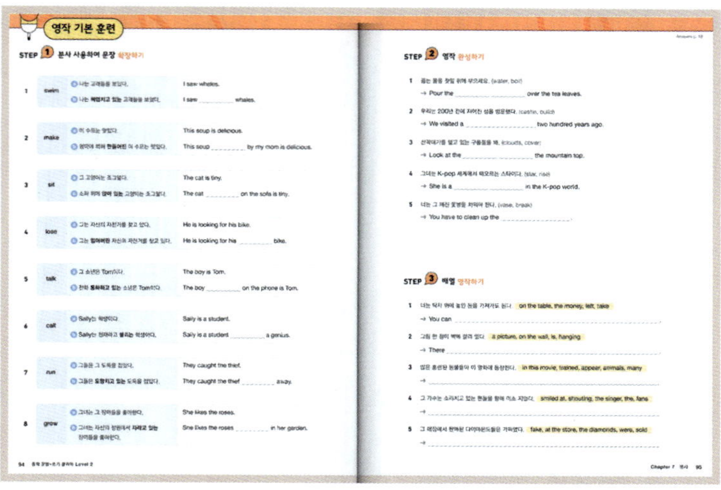

3단계 영작 기본 훈련

개념을 이해하며 쓰는 〈비교·확장하기 ▶ 영작 완성하기 ▶ 배열 영작하기〉의 3 STEP 훈련을 통해 영작의 기본기를 강화할 수 있습니다.

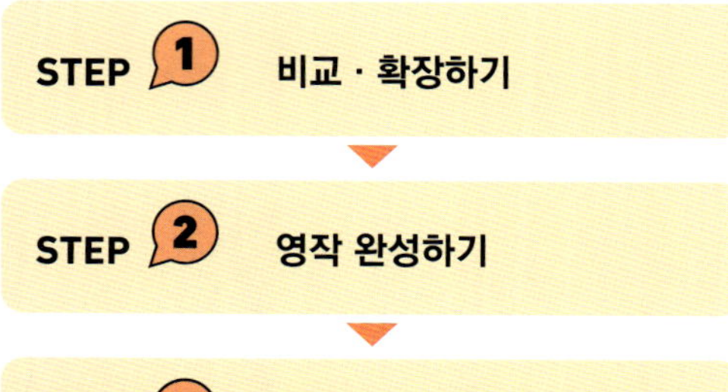

STEP **1** 비교 · 확장하기

STEP **2** 영작 완성하기

STEP **3** 배열 영작하기

❸ 

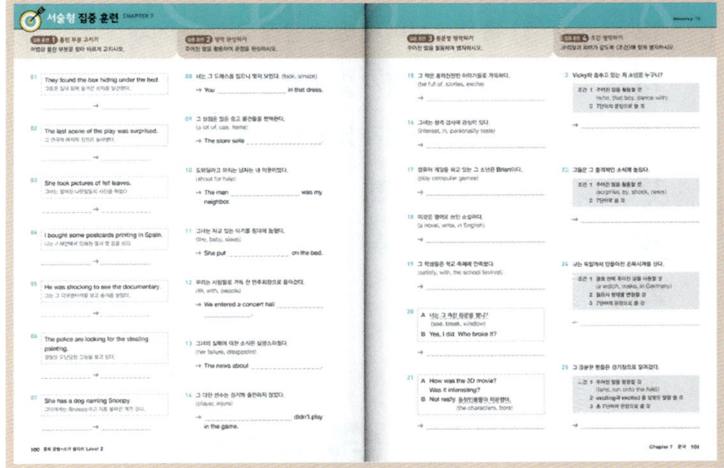

4가지 빈출 유형 서술형 집중 훈련

챕터별 4단계 집중 훈련을 통해 서술형 빈출 유형을 집중적으로 확실히 연습할 수 있습니다.

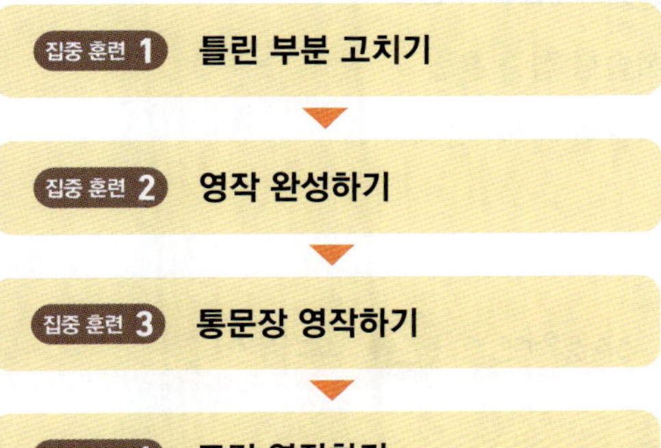

집중 훈련 **1** 틀린 부분 고치기

집중 훈련 **2** 영작 완성하기

집중 훈련 **3** 통문장 영작하기

집중 훈련 **4** 조건 영작하기

❹ 

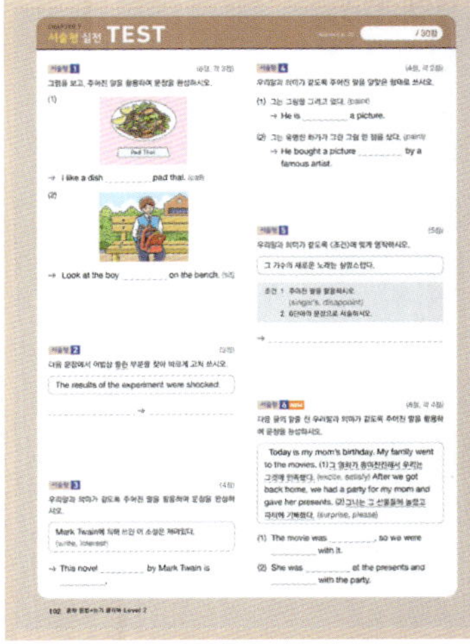

실전 유형으로 서술형 실전 TEST

체계적인 영작 훈련을 통해 쌓은 실력을 실전 유형에 적용해 보는 단계입니다.
학교 내신 시험에 출제되는 조건형·단락형·그림 서술형 문제 등 최신 서술형 유형을 골고루 배치하여 실전에 대비할 수 있습니다.

학교 내신 시험에 출제되는
다양한 유형의 문제를 풀어보며 챕터 완벽 마무리!

목차

시제

1 현재시제와 과거시제

A 현재시제는 현재의 상태, 반복적인 일이나 습관, 과학적 사실, 변함없는 진리 등을 나타낸다.

현재의 상태	My school **is** on a hill.
반복적인 일	They **go** to the movies every Sunday.
과학적 사실	The Earth **moves** around the Sun.

TIP 반복적인 일이나 현재의 습관을 나타내는 현재시제는 always(항상), usually(보통), sometimes(가끔)와 같은 빈도부사나 every Sunday(일요일마다), on weekends(주말마다)와 같은 표현과 주로 함께 쓴다.

B 과거시제는 과거에 일어난 일이나 과거의 상태, 역사적 사실을 나타낸다.

과거의 일·상태	Tom **met** Brian yesterday.
역사적 사실	Edison **invented** the light bulb in 1879.

TIP 과거시제는 yesterday, last week, two days ago, in 2020, then, at that time 등과 같이 과거의 특정 시점을 나타내는 말과 주로 함께 쓴다.

1 과거시제로 바꿔 쓰기

e.g. He comes. → He came.

1 I study. →

2 You sleep. →

3 We run. →

4 She dances. →

5 They go. →

6 Bill tries. →

7 The leaves fall. →

2 알맞은 시제의 동사 쓰기

1 live
We __________ in France two years ago.
We __________ in France now.

2 teach
Ms. Smith __________ English at a high school now.
Ms. Smith __________ English at a middle school last year.

3 eat
I __________ lunch with Lisa yesterday.
I __________ lunch alone these days.

 현재진행형과 과거진행형

현재 일어나고 있는 일은 현재진행형으로, 과거의 특정 시점에 일어나고 있었던 일은 과거진행형으로 나타낸다.

현재진행형	be동사의 현재형(am/are/is)+-ing	Sally **swims** every morning. ↓ Sally **is** **swimming** now.
과거진행형	be동사의 과거형(was/were)+-ing	Sally **swam** last Sunday. ↓ Sally **was** **swimming** at that time.

TIP 소유(have, own, belong to 등), 감정(like, love, hate 등), 인식(know, believe, understand 등)을 나타내는 동사는 진행형으로 쓰지 않는다.

I **have** a movie ticket. (○)   I am having a movie ticket. (×)

1 진행형 형태 익히기

1 sleep
그는 자고 있다. → He ___________ ___________.
그는 자고 있었다. → He ___________ ___________.

2 watch
우리는 영화를 보고 있다. → We ___________ ___________ a movie.
우리는 영화를 보고 있었다. → We ___________ ___________ a movie.

3 snow
눈이 아주 많이 오고 있다. → It ___________ ___________ heavily.
눈이 아주 많이 오고 있었다. → It ___________ ___________ heavily.

4 run
그들은 빨리 달리고 있다. → They ___________ ___________ fast.
그들은 빨리 달리고 있었다. → They ___________ ___________ fast.

2 진행형 형태 적용하기

보기	sit bake study climb

1 개미 몇 마리가 나무에 올라가고 있다. → Some ants ___________ ___________ up the tree.

2 그녀는 소파에 앉아 있었다. → She ___________ ___________ on the sofa.

3 나는 지금 쿠키를 굽고 있다. → I ___________ ___________ cookies now.

4 그들은 그때 수학을 공부하고 있었다. → They ___________ ___________ math at that time.

영작 기본 훈련

STEP 1 시제에 따른 의미 **비교하기**

1 take
- ⓐ 그는 어젯밤에 샤워를 **했다.**
  He __________ a shower last night.
- ⓑ 그는 매일 아침 샤워를 **한다.**
  He __________ a shower every morning.

2 boil
- ⓐ 물은 섭씨 100도에서 **끓는다.**
  Water __________ at 100℃.
- ⓑ 물이 지금 **끓고 있다.**
  Water __________ __________ now.

3 ring
- ⓐ 전화벨이 **울렸다.**
  The phone __________.
- ⓑ 전화벨이 그때 **울리고 있었다.**
  The phone __________ __________ at that time.

4 hold
- ⓐ 그 도시는 매년 그 축제를 **연다.**
  The city __________ the festival every year.
- ⓑ 그 도시는 작년에 그 축제를 **열었다.**
  The city __________ the festival last year.

5 exercise
- ⓐ 나는 체육관에서 **운동하고 있다.**
  I __________ __________ at the gym.
- ⓑ 나는 그때 체육관에서 **운동하고 있었다.**
  I __________ __________ at the gym at that time.

6 rise
- ⓐ 해가 어제 오전 7시에 **떴다.**
  The sun __________ at 7 a.m. yesterday.
- ⓑ 해가 지금 **뜨고 있다.**
  The sun __________ __________ now.

7 play
- ⓐ 그녀는 매일 아침 피아노를 **친다.**
  She __________ the piano every morning.
- ⓑ 그녀는 지금 피아노를 **치고 있다.**
  She __________ __________ the piano now.

8 get up
- ⓐ 나의 부모님은 어제 일찍 **일어나셨다.**
  My parents __________ __________ early yesterday.
- ⓑ 나의 부모님은 매일 일찍 **일어나신다.**
  My parents __________ __________ early every day.

STEP 2 영작 완성하기

| 보기 | buy | do | stay | know | arrive | open |

1 그 가게는 매일 아침 9시에 문을 연다.

→ The store _______________ at 9 a.m. every day.

2 우리는 그 당시 서울에 머무르고 있었다.

→ We _______________ in Seoul at that time.

3 그 선수들은 한 시간 전에 경기장에 도착했다.

→ The players _______________ at the stadium an hour ago.

4 나의 남동생은 지금 숙제를 하고 있다.

→ My brother _______________ his homework now.

5 나는 이 근처에 있는 좋은 제과점을 알고 있다.

→ I _______________ a nice bakery around here.

6 그는 어제 슈퍼마켓에서 이 사과들을 샀다.

→ He _______________ these apples at the supermarket yesterday.

STEP 3 문장 전환하기

1 Larry played badminton with his friends yesterday.

→ (현재시제) _______________________________________ every day.

2 The man is fixing a car now.

→ (과거진행형) _______________________________________ at that time.

3 I set the table an hour ago.

→ (현재진행형) _______________________________________ now.

4 They go to the amusement park every month.

→ (과거시제) _______________________________________ three months ago.

3 미래시제

A 미래시제는 앞으로 일어날 일이나 미래에 대한 예측을 나타낼 때 사용하며, 「will+동사원형」 또는 「be going to+동사원형」으로 쓴다.

Amy **will be** sixteen <u>next year</u>. ·······→ 미래시제는 tomorrow, next week, soon 등과 같이
It **is going to rain** <u>this weekend</u>. 미래의 시점을 나타내는 말과 주로 함께 쓴다.

B 말하는 시점에 결정한 일이나 주어의 의지를 나타낼 때는 「will+동사원형」을, 이미 예정된 계획을 나타낼 때는 「be going to+동사원형」을 주로 쓴다.

I**'ll call** you later. 〈말하는 시점에 결정함〉
I**'m going to leave** tomorrow. 〈내일 떠나기로 이미 계획함〉

1 미래시제 형태 익히기

e.g. 그는 공부할 것이다. (study) → _____He will study._____   _____He is going to study._____

1 우리는 점프할 것이다. (jump) → _______________   _______________

2 나는 잘 것이다. (sleep) → _______________   _______________

3 그녀는 노래할 것이다. (sing) → _______________   _______________

4 그들은 수영할 것이다. (swim) → _______________   _______________

2 미래시제 형태 적용하기

1 우리는 오후에 자전거를 탈 것이다. (ride)

→ We ___________ ___________ our bikes in the afternoon.

2 그녀는 내일 도서관에 있을 예정이다. (be)

→ She ___________ ___________ ___________ ___________ in the library tomorrow.

3 나는 다음 일요일에 그 식당에서 식사할 것이다. (eat)

→ I ___________ ___________ ___________ ___________ at that restaurant next Sunday.

4 그는 친구들을 자신의 생일 파티에 초대할 것이다. (invite)

→ He ___________ ___________ his friends to his birthday party.

 **미래시제의 부정문과 의문문**

A 「will+동사원형」의 부정문은 will not〔won't〕를 사용하고, 의문문은 will을 주어 앞으로 보내서 만든다.

부정문	will not〔won't〕+동사원형	Eric **will not〔won't〕 come** here tomorrow.
의문문	Will+주어+동사원형 ~?	**Will** Eric **come** here tomorrow? - Yes, he will. / No, he won't.

B 「be going to+동사원형」의 부정문은 be동사 뒤에 not을 쓰고, 의문문은 be동사를 주어 앞으로 보내서 만든다.

부정문	be동사+not+going to+동사원형	**I'm not going to buy** a new smartphone.
의문문	Be동사+주어+going to+동사원형 ~?	**Are** you **going to buy** a new smartphone? - Yes, I am. / No, I'm not.

1 미래시제 부정문과 의문문 형태 익히기

1 They will finish the project next month.

→ (부정문) They _________ _________ _________ the project next month.

→ (의문문) _________ _________ _________ the project next month?

2 We are going to take the test tomorrow.

→ (부정문) We _________ _________ _________ _________ _________ the test tomorrow.

→ (의문문) _________ _________ _________ _________ _________ the test tomorrow?

3 She is going to wear blue jeans this weekend.

→ (부정문) She _________ _________ _________ _________ blue jeans this weekend.

→ (의문문) _________ _________ _________ _________ _________ blue jeans this weekend?

4 He will clean his room by himself.

→ (부정문) He _________ _________ his room by himself.

→ (의문문) _________ _________ _________ his room by himself?

5 You are going to go to the beach tomorrow.

→ (부정문) You _________ _________ _________ _________ to the beach tomorrow.

→ (의문문) _________ _________ _________ _________ _________ to the beach tomorrow?

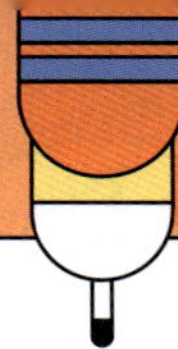

영작 기본 훈련

STEP 1 현재시제와 미래시제 비교하기

1 meet

ⓐ 그녀는 종종 그를 만난다.
She often __________ him.

ⓑ 그녀는 그를 만나지 않을 것이다.
She __________ __________ __________ him.

ⓒ 그녀는 그를 만날까?
__________ __________ __________ him?

2 jog

ⓐ 그는 조깅한다.
He __________.

ⓑ 그는 조깅할 것이다.
He __________ __________ __________ __________.

ⓒ 그는 조깅하지 않을 것이다.
He __________ __________ __________ __________ __________.

3 take

ⓐ 그들은 버스를 탄다.
They __________ the bus.

ⓑ 그들은 버스를 탈 것이다.
They __________ __________ __________ __________ the bus.

ⓒ 그들은 버스를 탈 거니?
__________ __________ __________ __________ the bus?

4 snow

ⓐ 매일 눈이 온다.
It __________ every day.

ⓑ 내일은 눈이 오지 않을 것이다.
It __________ __________ tomorrow.

ⓒ 내일 눈이 올까?
__________ __________ __________ tomorrow?

5 order

ⓐ 우리는 햄버거를 주문한다.
We __________ hamburgers.

ⓑ 우리는 햄버거를 주문할 것이다.
We __________ __________ __________ __________ hamburgers.

ⓒ 우리는 햄버거를 주문할 거니?
__________ __________ __________ __________ __________ hamburgers?

6 do

ⓐ 나는 숙제를 한다.
I __________ my homework.

ⓑ 나는 숙제를 할 것이다.
I'm __________ __________ __________ my homework.

ⓒ 나는 숙제를 하지 않을 것이다.
__________ __________ __________ __________ __________ my homework.

STEP **2** 문장 전환하기

e.g.	Kate will sit next to Bill.

→ Kate _____is_____ _____going_____ _____to_____ _____sit_____ next to Bill.

1 Ted and I will not play basketball.

→ Ted and I _______________ _______________ _______________ _______________ _______________ basketball.

2 Is he going to practice the piano tonight?

→ _______________ _______________ _______________ the piano tonight?

3 I'm not going to buy new clothes.

→ I _______________ _______________ new clothes.

4 Will Susan go on a picnic tomorrow?

→ _______________ _______________ _______________ _______________ _______________ on a picnic tomorrow?

STEP **3** 배열 영작하기

1 이번 주말에는 비가 오지 않을 것이다. not, rain, will, it

→ ____ this weekend.

2 너는 그 식당에 또 갈 거니? to, that restaurant, you, will, go

→ ____ again?

3 그는 전화번호를 바꾸지 않을 예정이다. going, not, change, is, his phone number, to, he

→ ____

4 우리는 그 축제를 준비할 것이다. the festival, we, prepare for, will

→ ____

5 너의 가족은 새집으로 이사할 예정이니? to, is, a new house, going, your family, move to

→ ____

A 과거의 일이 현재와 연관이 있거나 현재까지 영향을 미칠 때 현재완료형인 「have/has+p.p.」를 쓴다.

> 3년 전에는 살았지만 지금은 어떤지 알 수 없음

| 과거 | The man **lived** in the town three years ago. |
| 현재완료 | The man **has lived** in the town for three years. |

> 3년 전부터 지금까지 계속 살고 있음

TIP 현재완료는 yesterday, last ~, ~ ago와 같이 특정 과거 시점을 나타내는 부사(구)와 함께 쓸 수 없다.

He **stayed** in the hotel *two days ago*. (○)　　　He has stayed in the hotel *two days ago*. (×)

B 현재완료의 부정문은 have/has 뒤에 not(never)를 쓰고, 의문문은 Have/Has를 주어 앞으로 보내서 만든다.

| 부정문 | have/has+not+p.p. | He **has not(hasn't) come** home yet. |
| 의문문 | Have/Has+주어+p.p. ~? | **Have** you **seen** a ghost?
- Yes, I have. / No, I haven't. |

---

1 현재완료형 **쓰기**

e.g.	work	→ have worked		4	eat	→
1	buy	→		5	go	→
2	read	→		6	be	→
3	play	→		7	write	→

---

2 현재완료 **형태 익히기**

1 **see** 나는 전에 그 배우를 본 적이 있다. → I __________ __________ the actor before.

나는 전에 그 배우를 본 적이 없다. → I __________ __________ __________ the actor before.

2 **stay** 그들은 2020년부터 이곳에 머물러 왔다. → They __________ __________ here since 2020.

그들은 2020년부터 이곳에 머물러 왔니? → __________ they __________ here since 2020?

3 **meet** Linda는 이미 Tom을 만났다. → Linda __________ already __________ Tom.

Linda는 이미 Tom을 만났니? → __________ Linda already __________ Tom?

6 현재완료의 용법

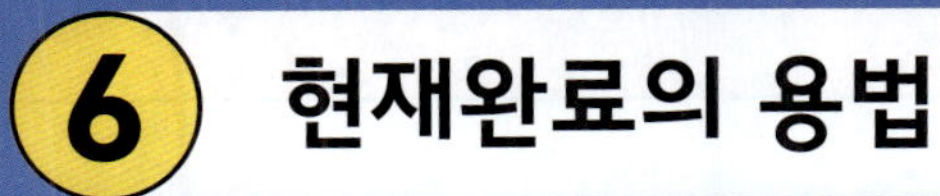

현재완료는 완료·경험·계속·결과의 의미를 나타낸다.

> 함께 자주 쓰이는 표현들

완료 (막 ~했다)	I **have** already **eaten** lunch.	just, already, yet 등
경험 (~한 적이 있다)	I **have been** to Jeju Island three times.	ever, never, before, once 등
계속 (~해 왔다)	We **have known** each other for two years.	for, since, how long 등
결과 (~해 버렸다)	I **have lost** my cell phone.	

cf. have been to는 '~에 가 본 적이 있다'는 의미이고, have gone to는 '~에 가 버렸다'는 의미이다.
They **have been to** Japan before. 그들은 전에 일본에 간 적이 있다. (가 보았던 경험)
They **have gone to** Japan. 그들은 일본에 가 버렸다. ('그래서 지금 여기 없다'는 결과)

1 현재완료 형태 적용하기

1 Sarah는 1년 동안 중국어를 공부해 왔다. (study)

→ Sarah ____________ ____________ Chinese for one year.

2 나는 저렇게 높은 건물을 본 적이 없다. (see, never)

→ I ____________ ____________ ____________ such a tall building.

3 소포가 이미 도착했다. (arrive)

→ The package __________ already __________.

4 우리는 몇 달 동안 서로를 알고 지내 왔다. (know)

→ We ____________ ____________ each other for a few months.

5 그 콘서트는 아직 시작하지 않았다. (start, not)

→ The concert __________ __________ __________ yet.

6 너는 스노클링을 해 본 적이 있니? (try)

→ __________ you ever __________ snorkeling?

7 Luna는 저녁 식사를 막 끝냈다. (finish)

→ Luna __________ just __________ dinner.

8 너는 내 블로그를 방문해 본 적이 있니? (visit)

→ __________ you ever __________ my blog?

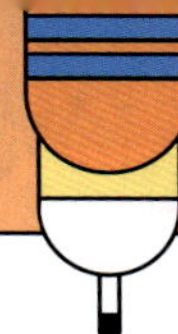

영작 기본 훈련

STEP 1 과거시제와 현재완료 비교하기

1 do
- ⓐ 나는 어제 숙제를 **했다**.   I _________ my homework yesterday.
- ⓑ 나는 막 숙제를 다 **했다**.   I _________ just _________ my homework.

2 work
- ⓐ Lora는 5년 전에 그곳에서 **일했다**.   Lora _________ there five years ago.
- ⓑ Lora는 5년 동안 그곳에서 **일해 왔다**.   Lora _________ _________ there for five years.

3 call
- ⓐ 그는 어젯밤에 내게 **전화하지 않았다**.   He _________ _________ me last night.
- ⓑ 그는 아직 내게 **전화하지 않았다**.   He _________ _________ _________ me yet.

4 read
- ⓐ 너는 언제 그 책을 **읽었니**?   When _________ you _________ the book?
- ⓑ 너는 그 책을 **읽은 적이 있니**?   _________ you ever _________ the book?

5 lose
- ⓐ 그녀는 지난달에 새 가방을 **잃어버렸다**.   She _________ her new bag last month.
- ⓑ 그녀는 새 가방을 **잃어버렸다**. (지금 그 가방이 없다.)   She _________ _________ her new bag.

6 meet
- ⓐ 우리는 어제 그를 **만나지 않았다**.   We _________ _________ him yesterday.
- ⓑ 우리는 한 번도 그를 **만난 적이 없다**.   We _________ never _________ him.

7 be
- ⓐ 직원들은 그때 **바빴다**.   The workers _________ busy then.
- ⓑ 직원들은 그때부터 **계속 바쁘다**.   The workers _________ _________ busy since then.

8 leave
- ⓐ 기차가 10분 전에 역을 **떠났니**?   _________ the train _________ the station ten minutes ago?
- ⓑ 기차가 이미 역을 **떠났니**?   _________ the train already _________ the station?

STEP **2** 영작 **완성하기**

e.g.
나는 버스에 우산을 두고 내렸다. (지금 우산이 없다.)
→ I ___*have*___ ___*left*___ my umbrella on the bus.

1 그 예술가는 2010년부터 파리에 산다.

→ The artist ___________ ___________ in Paris since 2010.

2 아버지가 막 전구를 교체하셨다.

→ My father ___________ just ___________ the light bulb.

3 내 생일은 이미 지났다.

→ My birthday ___________ already ___________.

4 Amy는 독일로 가 버렸다. (지금 여기 없다.)

→ Amy ___________ ___________ to Germany.

보기
pass
change
go
live
~~leave~~

STEP **3** 배열 **영작하기**

1 내 남동생은 지난 토요일부터 아프다. since, has, last Saturday, sick, been

→ My brother ____.

2 그들은 아직 여행에서 돌아오지 않았다. have, returned, from the trip, not, they

→ ____ yet.

3 너는 마술 쇼를 본 적이 있니? have, a magic show, you, seen, ever

→ ____

4 나는 5개월 동안 기타를 연주해 왔다. I, played, five months, the guitar, for, have

→ ____

5 그녀는 전에 멕시코 음식을 한 번도 먹어 본 적이 없다. never, has, before, she, Mexican food, eaten

→ ____

집중 훈련 1 틀린 부분 고치기
어법상 틀린 부분을 찾아 바르게 고치시오.

집중 훈련 2 영작 완성하기
주어진 말을 활용하여 문장을 완성하시오.

01

The film festival begins last weekend.
그 영화제는 지난 주말에 시작됐다.

______________ → ______________

02

Is he going to buying donuts at the bakery?
그는 그 제과점에서 도넛을 살 예정이니?

______________ → ______________

03

I am knowing Jina well.
나는 지나를 잘 알고 있다.

______________ → ______________

04

I had a headache since this morning.
나는 오늘 아침부터 계속 머리가 아프다.

______________ → ______________

05

They washing their car now.
그들은 지금 세차를 하고 있는 중이다.

______________ → ______________

06

They will do not their homework tomorrow.
그들은 내일 숙제를 하지 않을 것이다.

______________ → ______________

07

He saw this movie twice so far.
그는 지금까지 이 영화를 두 번 봤다.

______________ → ______________

08 그녀는 내 말을 듣고 있지 않았다. (listen)

→ She ____________________ to me.

09 나는 내일 이 책을 반납할 예정이다. (going, return)

→ I ____________________ this book
tomorrow.

10 Sam은 인도에 가 버렸다. (go)

→ Sam ____________________ to India.

11 그는 늘 식사 후에 이를 닦는다. (brush, his teeth)

→ He always ____________________ after
meals.

12 너는 얼마 동안 이 호텔에서 지내고 있니? (stay)

→ How long ____________________ in this
hotel?

13 그녀는 그 시험을 통과하지 못할 것이다. (pass, will)

→ She ____________________ the exam.

14 Sally는 이미 그 이메일을 보냈다.
(have, send, already)

→ Sally ____________________ the email.

집중 훈련 3 통문장 영작하기
주어진 말을 활용하여 영작하시오.

집중 훈련 4 조건 영작하기
우리말과 의미가 같도록 〈조건〉에 맞게 영작하시오.

15 Emma는 강아지 네 마리를 가지고 있다.
(have, puppies)

→ ___________________________

16 그들은 그곳에서 2년 동안 일해 왔다. (work, there, for)

→ ___________________________

17 Tom은 한 시간 전에 그림을 그리고 있었다.
(draw, a picture, ago)

→ ___________________________

18 너는 다음 달에 서울을 떠날 예정이니?
(going, leave, next month)

→ ___________________________

19 Jane은 어제 그녀의 자전거를 탔다. (ride, bike)

→ ___________________________

20

A 너는 내일 그에게 전화할 거니?
  (call, will, tomorrow)
B Yes, I will.

→ ___________________________

21

A 그는 유럽에 가 본 적이 있니?
  (be, to Europe)
B No, he hasn't.

→ ___________________________

22 그녀는 내일 수학을 공부하지 않을 예정이다.

조건 1 주어진 말을 사용할 것 (going, study math)
   2 부정 표현은 줄여 쓸 것
   3 7단어의 문장으로 서술할 것

→ ___________________________

23 John은 에펠탑을 본 적이 한 번도 없다.

조건 1 주어진 말을 활용할 것
   (see, the Eiffel Tower, never)
   2 7단어의 문장으로 쓸 것

→ ___________________________

24 Joe와 Amy는 그들의 개를 찾고 있었다.

조건 1 괄호 안에 주어진 말을 사용할 것
   (look for, dog)
   2 필요시 형태를 변형할 것
   3 모두 8단어로 쓸 것

→ ___________________________

25 Juile는 매일 아침 신문을 읽는다.

조건 1 read와 the newspaper를 사용할 것
   2 필요시 형태를 변형할 것
   3 6단어의 문장으로 쓸 것

→ ___________________________

서술형 **1**　　(2점, 각 1점)

다음 문장을 지시대로 바꿔 쓰시오.

(1) Chris has planned his vacation. (부정문으로)

→ _________________________________ yet.

(2) Chris is going to visit his grandparents.
(의문문으로)

→ _________________________________

서술형 **2**　　(4점, 각 2점)

우리말과 의미가 같도록 주어진 말을 활용하여 문장을 완성하시오.

(1) 그녀는 TV에서 음악 프로그램을 볼 것이다. (watch)

→ She __________ __________ a music
program on TV.

(2) 내 친구들은 역에서 나를 기다리고 있었다. (wait for)

→ My friends __________ __________
__________ __________ at the station.

서술형 **3**　　(6점, 각 3점)

그림을 보고, 주어진 말을 활용하여 문장을 완성하시오.

yesterday	today
go to the beach	make sandwiches

(1) Alex _________________________ yesterday.

(2) Alex _________________________ right now.

서술형 **4**　　(9점, 각 3점)

〈보기〉의 단어를 알맞은 형태로 바꿔 문장을 완성하시오.

보기	teach	hear	arrive

(1) Linda __________ at the airport an hour ago.

(2) __________ he __________ children since
2022?

(3) I __________ never __________ the story
before.

서술형 **5**　　(3점)

다음 문장에서 어법상 틀린 부분을 찾아 바르게 고쳐 쓰시오.

Sarah is having lots of lovely dolls.

__________________ → __________________

서술형 **6** NEW　　(6점, 각 2점)

Tom의 일과 계획표를 보고, 주어진 말을 활용하여 문장을 완성하시오.

11:30 a.m.	eat out with Mom and Dad
2:00 p.m.	go to the library with Joe
7:00 p.m.	take a walk in the park

(1) Tom _____________________ with his
parents at 11:30 a.m. (be going to)

(2) Tom and Joe _____________________ to
the library at 2:00 p.m. (be going to)

(3) Tom _____________________ in the park
at 7:00 p.m. (will)

조동사

1 can, may

2 must, have to

3 should, had better

4 used to, would like to

A can은 능력·가능, 허가, 요청, 추측의 의미를 나타낸다.

능력·가능	~할 수 있다	Judy **can** play the guitar. I **can** come to the party.
허가	~해도 된다	You **can** fly drones here. **Can** I use your phone?
요청	~해 주겠니?	**Can** you show me the way?
부정적 추측	~일 리 없다	The story **cannot**〔**can't**〕 be true.

요청을 나타낼 때 could를 쓰면 더 정중한 표현이 된다.

cf. 능력·가능을 나타내는 can은 be able to로 바꿔 쓸 수 있으며, be동사는 주어의 인칭과 수, 문장의 시제에 맞춰 쓴다.
　　 She **was able to** arrive here before dark.

B may는 허가나 약한 추측의 의미를 나타낸다.

허가	~해도 된다	You **may** keep this book. You **may not** sit here. **May** I leave now?
약한 추측	~일지도 모른다	He **may** know Jane.

허가를 나타내는 may의 부정은 '~하면 안 된다'라는 의미이다.

---

1 **can과 may** 형태 익히기

1 수영할 수 있다　→ _________ swim

　　수영할 수 없다　→ _________ _________

2 올지도 모른다　→ _________ come

　　안 올지도 모른다　→ _________ _________ _________

2 알맞은 조동사를 사용하여 문장 완성하기 (<보기>의 표현을 한 번씩만 쓸 것)

1 제가 난방기를 꺼도 될까요? (turn)

　→ _________ I _________ off the heater?

2 나에게 소금을 건네주겠니? (pass)

　→ _________ you _________ me the salt?

3 그는 피곤할 리가 없다. (be)

　→ He _________ _________ tired.

4 나는 어려운 문제들을 풀 수 있다. (solve)

　→ I _________ _________ _________ _________ difficult problems.

> ┤ 보기 ├
>
> can
> can't
> be able to
> may

② must, have to

A must는 강한 의무나 추측의 의미를 나타내며, 부정형 must not은 금지를 나타낸다.

강한 의무	~해야 한다	You **must** wear a helmet.
금지	~하면 안 된다	You **must not** enter the room.
강한 추측	~임이 틀림없다	She **must** be at school now.

B 의무를 나타내는 must는 have/has to로 바꿔 쓸 수 있으며, 부정형 don't/doesn't have to는 불필요를 나타낸다.

| 강한 의무 | ~해야 한다 | Linda **has to** finish her homework. |
| 불필요 | ~할 필요가 없다 | Joe **doesn't have to** go to bed early today. |

cf. 조동사 must의 과거형은 had to를, 미래형은 will have to를 쓴다.

I **had to** get up early yesterday.　　　They **will have to** leave tomorrow.

---

1 must와 have to 형태 익히기

1　먹어야 한다　　　　　　→ ___________ eat

　　먹으면 안 된다　　　　　→ ___________ ___________ ___________

2　줄을 서야 한다　　　　　→ ___________ ___________ stand in line

　　줄을 설 필요가 없다　　→ ___________ ___________ ___________ ___________ in line

3　친절해야 한다　　　　　→ ___________ ___________ be kind

　　친절함이 틀림없다　　　→ ___________ ___________ kind

2 must와 have to를 사용하여 문장 완성하기

1　이 결과들은 잘못된 것임이 틀림없다. (be)

　→ These results ___________ ___________ wrong.

2　Stella는 그녀의 어머니를 도와야 한다. (help)

　→ Stella ___________ ___________ ___________ her mother.

3　우리는 이곳에서 사진을 찍어서는 안 된다. (take)

　→ We ___________ ___________ ___________ photos here.

4　그들은 벽을 다시 페인트칠해야 했다. (paint)

　→ They ___________ ___________ ___________ the wall again.

STEP ❶ 조동사 의미 비교하기

1
- ⓐ 우리는 문을 **닫아야 한다.** — We must close the door.
- ⓑ 우리는 문을 **닫으면 안 된다.** — We __________ __________ __________ the door.
- ⓒ 우리는 문을 **닫을 필요가 없다.** — We __________ __________ __________ __________ the door.

2
- ⓐ 그것은 **사실일지도 모른다.** — It may be true.
- ⓑ 그것은 **사실임이 틀림없다.** — It __________ __________ true.
- ⓒ 그것은 **사실일 리가 없다.** — It __________ __________ true.

3
- ⓐ 그녀는 책상을 **옮길 수 있다.** — She can move the desk.
- ⓑ 그녀는 책상을 **옮길 수 없다.** — She __________ __________ the desk.
- ⓒ 그녀는 책상을 **옮길 수 없었다.** — She __________ __________ __________ __________ the desk.

4
- ⓐ 너는 여기에서 **기다려도 된다.** — You may wait here.
- ⓑ 제가 여기에서 **기다려도 되나요?** — __________ I __________ here?
- ⓒ 여기에서 **기다려 주겠어요?** — __________ you __________ here?

5
- ⓐ James는 파스타를 **요리해야 한다.** — James has to cook pasta.
- ⓑ James는 파스타를 **요리할 필요가 없다.** — James __________ __________ __________ __________ pasta.
- ⓒ James는 파스타를 **요리해야 하나요?** — __________ James __________ __________ __________ pasta?

6
- ⓐ 그는 그곳에 **가야 한다.** — He has to go there.
- ⓑ 그는 그곳에 **가야 했다.** — He __________ __________ __________ there.
- ⓒ 그는 그곳에 **갈 필요가 없었다.** — He __________ __________ __________ __________ there.

STEP 2 영작 완성하기

| 보기 | finish | feed | lose | be | know |

1 우리는 결승전에서 패할지도 모른다.

→ We ___________ ___________ the final match.

2 그는 이 질문에 대한 답을 아는 것이 틀림없다.

→ He ___________ ___________ the answer to this question.

3 너는 제시간에 그 일을 끝낼 수 있니?

→ ___________ you ___________ the work on time?

4 Amy는 학교에 지각할 리가 없다.

→ Amy ___________ ___________ late for school.

5 그녀는 매일 그녀의 개에게 먹이를 줘야 한다.

→ She ___________ ___________ ___________ her dog every day.

STEP 3 배열 영작하기

1 학생들은 시험 중에 소리를 내서는 안 된다.　must, make noise, not, students

→ ____ during the test.

2 나의 삼촌은 그 차를 고칠 수 있었다.　able, the car, was, repair, to

→ My uncle ____.

3 그녀는 2주 안에 돌아오지 않을지도 모른다.　may, come, in two weeks, back, not

→ She ____.

4 너는 독후감을 쓸 필요가 없다.　have, a book report, to, don't, write

→ You ____.

5 제가 이 컴퓨터를 사용해도 될까요?　I, this computer, use, may

→ ____

A   should는 의무나 충고·조언의 의미를 나타낸다.

의무	~해야 한다
충고·조언	~하는 것이 좋다

We **should** recycle paper.
You **should not**(**shouldn't**) lie to your parents.

You **should** drink more water.

B   had better는 강한 충고나 권고의 의미를 나타낸다.

충고·권고	~하는 것이 낫다〔좋겠다〕

You **had better** hurry.
You **had better** **not** go there.

         not의 위치에 유의한다.

1   should와 had better 의미 익히기

e.g. should wear	→ 입어야 한다		3	had better stop	→
1 should be kind	→		**4**	had better leave	→
2 should not run	→		**5**	had better not forget	→

2   should와 had better 형태 적용하기

보기	do	run	see	spread

1   우리는 모든 일에 최선을 다해야 한다.

→ We ___________ ___________ our best in everything.

2   그들은 나에 대한 소문을 퍼뜨리지 않는 게 좋다.

→ They ___________ ___________ ___________ ___________ rumors about me.

3   너는 의사의 진찰을 받는 게 좋겠다.

→ You ___________ ___________ ___________ a doctor.

4   너희들은 교실에서 뛰어다니면 안 된다.

→ You ___________ ___________ ___________ around in the classroom.

 **used to, would like to**

A used to는 과거의 습관이나 상태를 나타낸다. 과거의 습관을 나타낼 때는 would로 바꿔 쓸 수 있다.

| 과거의 습관 | ~하곤 했다(= would) | We **used to** go camping on weekends.
= We **would** go camping on weekends. |
| 과거의 상태 | ~이었다 | The man **used to** be a taxi driver.
There **used to** be a big tree in the garden. |

cf. 「be used to+-ing」는 '~하는 데 익숙하다'라는 의미이다.
We **are used to watching** videos on our smartphones.

used to는 '(과거에는) ~했으나 지금은 더 이상 그렇지 않다'는 뜻을 포함한다.

B would like to는 소망을 나타낸다.

| 소망 | ~하고 싶다 | I **would**(**I'd**) **like to** have some juice. |

would는 'd로 줄여 쓸 수 있다.

---

1 used to와 would like to 형태 익히기

1 Jeff는 어제 운동했다. (exercise) → Jeff ___________ yesterday.

Jeff는 아침에 운동하곤 했다. → Jeff ___________ ___________ ___________ in the morning.

2 나는 주말에 집에 있는다. (stay) → I ___________ home on the weekends.

나는 오늘 집에 있고 싶다. → I ___________ ___________ ___________ ___________ home today.

2 used to와 would like to 형태 적용하기

| 보기 | join | take | ask | be |

1 저는 그 동아리에 가입하고 싶습니다.

→ I ___________ ___________ ___________ ___________ the club.

2 Brown 씨는 유명한 피아노 연주자였다.

→ Mr. Brown ___________ ___________ ___________ a famous pianist.

3 Harry는 동물 사진을 찍곤 했다.

→ Harry ___________ ___________ ___________ pictures of animals.

4 우리는 너에게 질문을 하나 하고 싶다.

→ We ___________ ___________ ___________ ___________ you a question.

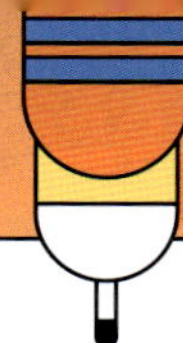

영작 기본 훈련

STEP 1 조동사 의미 **비교하기**

1
- **a** 너는 휴식을 취해도 된다.　　You can take a break.
- **b** 너는 휴식을 취해야 한다.　　You _________ _________ a break.
- **c** 너는 휴식을 취하는 게 좋겠다.　　You _________ _________ _________ a break.

2
- **a** 우리는 축구를 할 수 없다.　　We can't play soccer.
- **b** 우리는 축구를 하고 싶다.　　We _________ _________ _________ _________ soccer.
- **c** 우리는 축구를 하곤 했다.　　We _________ _________ _________ soccer.

3
- **a** 나는 비밀번호를 바꿀지도 모른다.　　I may change the password.
- **b** 나는 비밀번호를 바꾸는 게 좋겠다.　　I _________ _________ _________ the password.
- **c** 나는 비밀번호를 바꾸고 싶다.　　I _________ _________ _________ _________ the password.

4
- **a** 너는 늦게까지 깨어 있어야 한다.　　You should stay up late.
- **b** 너는 늦게까지 깨어 있으면 안 된다.　　You _________ _________ _________ up late.
- **c** 너는 늦게까지 깨어 있지 않는 게 좋겠다.　　You _________ _________ _________ _________ up late.

5
- **a** 그녀는 쿠키를 좀 구워야 한다.　　She has to bake some cookies.
- **b** 그녀를 쿠키를 좀 굽고 싶어 한다.　　She _________ _________ _________ _________ some cookies.
- **c** 그녀는 방과 후에 쿠키를 굽곤 했다.　　She _________ _________ cookies after school.

6
- **a** 이곳이 식당일 리가 없다.　　This place can't be a restaurant.
- **b** 이곳은 식당이었다.　　This place _________ _________ _________ a restaurant.
- **c** 이곳은 식당임이 틀림없다.　　This place _________ _________ a restaurant.

STEP ② 영작 완성하기

| 보기 |　　would　　　had better　　　would like to　　　used to　　　should |

1　아이들은 채소를 더 많이 먹어야 한다. (eat)

➡ Children __________ __________ more vegetables.

2　이곳에 작은 교회가 있었다. (be)

➡ There __________ __________ __________ a small church here.

3　나는 차가운 무언가를 마시고 싶다. (drink)

➡ I __________ __________ __________ __________ something cold.

4　그는 주말이면 아버지와 하이킹을 가곤 했다. (go)

➡ He __________ __________ hiking with his father on weekends.

5　너는 우리에게 거짓말하지 않는 것이 좋다. (lie)

➡ You __________ __________ __________ __________ to us.

STEP ③ 배열 영작하기

1　우리는 공원에 있는 꽃을 꺾으면 안 된다.　should, flowers, in the park, not, pick

➡ We ____.

2　Jessy는 Andy와 같은 학교에 다녔다.　used, the same, go to, school, to

➡ Jessy ____________________________________ as Andy.

3　너는 안전벨트를 매는 게 좋다.　your seat belt, had, wear, better

➡ You ____.

4　나는 기차를 타고 유럽 여기저기를 여행하고 싶다.　would, around Europe, to, I, travel, like

➡ ____ by train.

5　너는 지금 당장은 그에게 전화하지 않는 게 낫겠다.　not, better, you, call, had, him

➡ ____ right now.

집중 훈련 1 틀린 부분 고치기
어법이나 의미가 틀린 부분을 찾아 바르게 고치시오.

집중 훈련 2 영작 완성하기
주어진 말을 활용하여 문장을 완성하시오.

01 He may comes back tomorrow.
그는 내일 돌아올지도 모른다.

__________ → __________

02 She has better apologize to her friend.
그녀는 친구에게 사과하는 것이 좋겠다.

__________ → __________

03 You must not wash the dishes.
너는 설거지를 할 필요가 없다.

__________ → __________

04 We are not able to sleep at all last night.
우리는 어젯밤에 한숨도 잘 수 없었다.

__________ → __________

05 They can be very hungry now.
그들은 지금 매우 배고픈 것임이 틀림없다.

__________ → __________

06 She was used to play tennis after school.
그녀는 방과 후에 테니스를 치곤 했다.

__________ → __________

07 May you tell me your address?
당신의 주소를 제게 말해 주시겠어요?

__________ → __________

08 나는 이 요가 수업을 듣고 싶다. (would, take)

→ __________________ this yoga class.

09 너는 박물관에 있는 그림들을 만지면 안 된다. (touch)

→ __________________ the paintings in the museum.

10 나의 할아버지는 경찰관이셨다.
(used, a police officer)

→ My grandfather ________________.

11 너는 돈을 좀 모으는 것이 좋겠다.
(save, some money)

→ You ________________.

12 제가 이제 자리에 앉아도 되나요? (take a seat)

→ __________________ now?

13 Suzie는 어젯밤에 9시까지 집에 와야 했다.
(come home)

→ Suzie ________________ by 9 last night.

14 이것이 네 책일 리가 없다. (be)

→ This ________________.

집중 훈련 3 통문장 영작하기
주어진 말을 활용하여 영작하시오.

15 너희들은 점심 식사를 하러 나가도 된다.
(go out, for lunch)

→ _______________________________

16 그는 토요일마다 체육관에 가곤 했다.
(go to the gym, on Saturdays)

→ _______________________________

17 그녀는 Eric의 엄마임이 틀림없다. (be, Eric's mom)

→ _______________________________

18 그는 자신의 노트북을 가져오지 않을지도 모른다.
(bring, his laptop)

→ _______________________________

19 나는 저 나무 아래에서 쉬고 싶다.
(like, rest, under that tree)

→ _______________________________

20
A 지금 당신과 이야기해도 될까요?
　　(talk to, now)
B Of course you can. I'm not busy.

→ _______________________________

21
A I'm so busy writing my report.
B Relax. 너는 그것을 오늘 밤에 끝낼 필요가 없어.
　　(have to, finish, tonight)

→ _______________________________

집중 훈련 4 조건 영작하기
우리말과 의미가 같도록 〈조건〉에 맞게 영작하시오.

22 Henry는 그의 차를 팔아야 한다.

조건 **1** 주어진 말을 모두 사용할 것
　　　(have, sell, car)
　　 2 필요시 형태를 변형할 것
　　 3 6단어의 문장으로 쓸 것

→ _______________________________

23 그들은 작년에는 한국어를 말할 수 없었다.

조건 **1** 〈보기〉의 표현을 모두 사용할 것
　　 2 부정 표현은 줄여 쓸 것
　　 3 8단어의 문장으로 쓸 것

보기　　able　　speak Korean　　last year

→ _______________________________

24 Jennifer는 오늘 학교에 갈 필요가 없다.

조건 **1** 괄호 안에 주어진 말을 사용할 것
　　　(have, go to school)
　　 2 줄임말을 사용할 것
　　 3 모두 8단어로 쓸 것

→ _______________________________

25 너는 자기 전에 아무것도 먹지 않는 게 좋겠다.

조건 **1** eat, anything, before bed를 사용할 것
　　 2 총 8단어의 문장으로 쓸 것

→ _______________________________

서술형 **1**　(10점, 각 2점)

〈보기〉에 주어진 조동사와 동사를 <u>한 번씩</u> 사용하여 문장을 완성하시오.

보기	must	be
	used to	skip
	shouldn't	hurry
	would like to	watch
	had better	take walks

(1) You _________________________ breakfast.
　 It's not good for your health.

(2) This new movie looks very interesting.
　 I _________________________ it with you.

(3) Jane sings very well.
　 She _________________________ a singer.

(4) Rosa _________________________.
　 She may miss the school bus.

(5) Roy _________________________ after dinner.
　 He doesn't anymore.

서술형 **2**　(8점, 각 4점)

다음 대화의 밑줄 친 우리말과 의미가 같도록 알맞은 조동사와 주어진 말을 사용하여 대화를 완성하시오.

> (1) **A** <u>나에게 연필을 빌려주겠니?</u> (lend)
> 　 **B** Sure. Here you are.

→ _________________________ me a pencil?

> (2) **A** Did you enjoy the musical?
> 　 **B** No. <u>우리는 표를 살 수 없었어.</u> (buy tickets)
> 　　 It was sold out.

→ _________________________

서술형 **3**　(2점)

우리말과 의미가 같도록 문장을 완성하시오.

> 나의 학교 앞에는 작은 호수가 있었다.

→ There _________ _________ _________
　 a small lake in front of my school.

서술형 **4**　(6점, 각 3점)

우리말과 의미가 같도록 〈보기〉에서 알맞은 조동사를 골라 주어진 말을 사용하여 영작하시오.

보기	cannot	must not	don't have to

(1) 저 소년은 Danny일 리가 없다. (that boy)
　 → _________________________

(2) 우리는 시간을 낭비하면 안 된다. (waste time)
　 → _________________________

서술형 **5**　(4점)

다음 대화의 밑줄 친 ①~⑤ 중 흐름상 <u>어색한</u> 부분을 찾아 바르게 고치시오.

> **Betty** What time does the concert begin?
> **Joe** It begins at 7:30.
> **Betty** ① <u>Do we have to be there before 7:00?</u>
> **Joe** We ② <u>have to</u>. We ③ <u>should</u> be there by 7:15.
> **Betty** Okay. ④ <u>May I bring a camera?</u>
> **Joe** Of course. But you ⑤ <u>must not</u> take photos during the concert.

→ _________________________

수동태

A 주어가 행위의 주체일 때는 능동태로, 주어가 행위의 대상일 때는 수동태로 나타낸다.

| 능동태 | Many teenagers **watch** this show. 〈주어(Many teenagers)가 행위(watch)의 주체〉 |
| 수동태 | This show **is watched** by many teenagers. 〈주어(This show)가 행위(watch)의 대상〉 |

B 수동태는 「be동사+p.p.」의 형태로 '~되다(받다/당하다)'의 의미이다.

| Many people | **love** | this song. |

This song | **is loved** | **by** many people.

→ 수동태 문장에서 행위자는 「by + 목적격」으로 나타낸다.

→ be동사는 주어의 인칭과 수, 시제에 맞춘다.

1 능동태와 수동태 형태 구분하기

1 clean

Anna는 교실을 청소한다. → Anna ＿＿＿＿＿＿ the classroom.

교실은 Anna에 의해 청소된다. → The classroom ＿＿＿＿＿＿ by Anna.

2 use

젊은이들은 공공 자전거를 이용한다. → Young people ＿＿＿＿＿＿ public bikes.

공공 자전거는 젊은이들에 의해 이용된다. → Public bikes ＿＿＿＿＿＿ by young people.

3 fix

그는 매일 많은 차들을 수리한다. → He ＿＿＿＿＿＿ a lot of cars every day.

많은 차들이 매일 그에 의해 수리된다. → A lot of cars ＿＿＿＿＿＿ by him every day.

2 수동태 형태 적용하기

1 이 식당의 음식은 한 유명한 주방장에 의해 요리된다. (cook)

→ This restaurant's food ＿＿＿＿＿ ＿＿＿＿＿ by a famous chef.

2 저 성들은 매년 많은 관광객들에 의해 방문된다. (visit)

→ Those castles ＿＿＿＿＿ ＿＿＿＿＿ by many tourists each year.

3 전교 회장은 학생들에 의해 선출된다. (elect)

→ The school president ＿＿＿＿＿ ＿＿＿＿＿ by students.

4 이 트럭들은 우리에 의해 주말마다 세차된다. (wash)

→ These trucks ＿＿＿＿＿ ＿＿＿＿＿ by us every weekend.

2 수동태의 시제

수동태의 시제는 be동사를 시제에 맞게 바꾸어 나타낸다.

현재시제	am/are/is+p.p.	These baskets **are made** by local people.
과거시제	was/were+p.p.	The building **was built** in 2000.
미래시제	will be+p.p.	The room **will be painted** by Alice.

TIP 수동태 문장에서 행위자를 알 수 없거나 언급할 필요가 없을 때는 「by+목적격」을 생략할 수 있다.

The island **was found** twenty years ago.
A lot of birds **are seen** near the river.

1 수동태의 시제 익히기

1 나는
- 초대받는다. (invite) → I ___________ ___________.
- 초대받았다. → I ___________ ___________.
- 초대받을 것이다. → I ___________ ___________ ___________.

2 도구들이
- 만들어진다. (make) → Tools ___________ ___________.
- 만들어졌다. → Tools ___________ ___________.
- 만들어질 것이다. → Tools ___________ ___________ ___________.

2 시제에 맞는 수동태 형태 적용하기

1 그 초대장들은 내 비서에 의해 보내질 것이다. (send)

→ The invitations ___________ ___________ ___________ by my secretary.

2 고장 난 컴퓨터들은 대개 24시간 내에 수리된다. (repair)

→ Broken computers ___________ usually ___________ within 24 hours.

3 이 교과서들은 온라인에서 구입되었다. (buy)

→ These textbooks ___________ ___________ online.

4 내 가방은 파란색 셔츠를 입은 남자에 의해 도난당했다. (steal)

→ My bag ___________ ___________ by a man in a blue shirt.

5 꽃들은 호수 주위에 심어질 것이다. (plant)

→ Flowers ___________ ___________ ___________ around the lake.

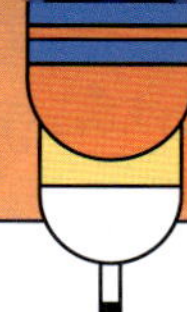

영작 기본 훈련

1 hold

ⓐ 그들은 매년 그 축제를 **연다**.
They __________ the festival every year.

ⓑ 그 축제는 매년 **열린다**.
The festival __________ __________ every year.

2 write

ⓐ Alex가 이 시들을 **썼다**.
Alex __________ these poems.

ⓑ 이 시들은 Alex에 의해 **쓰였다**.
These poems __________ __________ __________ Alex.

3 catch

ⓐ 경찰이 그 도둑들을 **잡을 것이다**.
The police __________ __________ the thieves.

ⓑ 그 도둑들은 경찰에게 **잡힐 것이다**.
The thieves __________ __________ __________ __________ the police.

4 sell

ⓐ 우리는 스포츠카를 **판매한다**.
We __________ sports cars.

ⓑ 스포츠카는 **우리에 의해 판매된다**.
Sports cars __________ __________ __________ __________.

5 design

ⓐ 나는 그 웹사이트를 **설계할 것이다**.
I __________ __________ the website.

ⓑ 그 웹사이트는 나에 의해 **설계될 것이다**.
The website __________ __________ __________ __________ me.

6 bite

ⓐ 그 개가 그 소년을 **물었다**.
The dog __________ the boy.

ⓑ 그 소년은 그 개에게 **물렸다**.
The boy __________ __________ __________ the dog.

7 make

ⓐ 로봇들이 이 장난감들을 **만든다**.
Robots __________ these toys.

ⓑ 이 장난감들은 로봇들에 의해 **만들어진다**.
These toys __________ __________ __________ robots.

8 break

ⓐ 그녀가 그 컵을 **깼다**.
She __________ the cup.

ⓑ 그 컵은 **그녀에 의해 깨졌다**.
The cup __________ __________ __________ __________.

STEP **2** 문장 전환하기

1 A famous cartoonist drew this cartoon.

→ This cartoon ____.

2 Mr. Green bakes strawberry cakes every Sunday.

→ ____ every Sunday.

3 A car hit the bird last night.

→ ____ last night.

4 My grandparents grow beautiful roses in their garden.

→ ____ in their garden.

5 He will solve the difficult problem.

→ ____

STEP **3** 배열 영작하기

1 우리의 일정이 변경될 것이다. will, our schedule, changed, be

→ ____

2 이 벽은 자원봉사자들에 의해 칠해졌다. painted, by, this wall, volunteers, was

→ ____

3 대부분의 석유는 중동에서 생산된다. the Middle East, produced, in, is, most oil

→ ____

4 내 휴대 전화는 베개 밑에서 발견되었다. was, the pillow, my cell phone, found, under

→ ____

5 그 프로젝트는 Tony에 의해 관리될 것이다. will, Tony, by, be, the project, managed

→ ____

3 수동태 문장의 다양한 형태

A 수동태의 부정문은 be동사 뒤에 not을 붙이고, 의문문은 be동사를 주어 앞으로 보내서 만든다.

부정문	be동사+not+p.p.	Some words **are not used** today.
의문문	Be동사+주어+p.p. ~?	**Was** this book **written** by Mark Twain?
	의문사+be동사+주어+p.p. ~?	**When was** this book **written**?

B 조동사가 있는 수동태는 「조동사+be+p.p.」의 형태로 쓴다.

The flight **may be delayed**. 　　　　비행이 지연될지도 모른다.
The alarm **must be set** for 6 a.m. 　　알람은 오전 6시에 맞춰져야 한다.

1 수동태의 부정문과 의문문 형태 익히기

1 너의 이메일이
- 보내졌다. (send) → Your email _________ _________.
- 보내지지 않았다. → Your email _________ _________ _________.
- 보내졌니? → _________ your email _________?

2 그 쿠키들은
- 매일 구워진다. (bake) → The cookies _________ _________ every day.
- 매일 구워지지는 않는다. → The cookies _________ _________ _________ every day.
- 매일 구워지니? → _________ the cookies _________ every day?

3 그 사진은
- 그날 찍혔다. (take) → The photo _________ _________ that day.
- 그날 찍히지 않았다. → The photo _________ _________ _________ that day.
- 언제 찍혔니? → _________ _________ the photo _________?

2 조동사가 있는 수동태 익히기

1 그 문제는 해결될 수 있다. (solve)

→ The problem ___________ ___________ ___________.

2 소포들은 저녁에 배달될지도 모른다. (deliver)

→ Packages ___________ ___________ ___________ in the evening.

3 모두가 법에 의해 보호받아야 한다. (protect)

→ Everyone ___________ ___________ ___________ by law.

 4   by 이외의 전치사를 쓰는 수동태

수동태 문장에서 행위자는 보통 by와 함께 쓰지만, by 이외의 전치사를 쓰는 경우도 있다.

be filled with	~로 가득 차다	be worried about	~에 대해 걱정하다
be covered with	~로 덮여 있다	be pleased with	~에 기뻐하다
be interested in	~에 관심이 있다	be satisfied with	~에 만족하다
be scared of	~을 무서워하다	be surprised at(by)	~에 놀라다
be crowded with	~로 붐비다	be known as	~로 알려져 있다

The jar **is filled with** colorful shells.
We **were surprised at** the news.

---

1   by 이외의 전치사를 쓰는 수동태 형태 익히기

| 보기 | know   scare   fill   satisfy   ~~cover~~ |

e.g.   먼지로 덮여 있다 → be _covered_ _with_ dust

1   거미를 무서워하다 → be ____________ ____________ spiders

2   천재로 알려져 있다 → be ____________ ____________ a genius

3   그 결정에 만족하다 → be ____________ ____________ the decision

4   책들로 가득 차다 → be ____________ ____________ books

2   by 이외의 전치사를 쓰는 수동태 문장 완성하기

1   캠핑하는 사람들은 주말 날씨에 대해 걱정한다. (worry)

  → Campers ____________ ____________ ____________ the weekend weather.

2   그 쇼핑몰은 내일 쇼핑하는 사람들로 붐빌 것이다. (crowd)

  → The mall ____________ ____________ ____________ ____________ shoppers tomorrow.

3   Rachel은 그 광경에 놀라지 않았다. (surprise)

  → Rachel ____________ ____________ ____________ ____________ the sight.

4   너는 K-pop 음악에 관심이 있니? (interest)

  → ____________ you ____________ ____________ K-pop music?

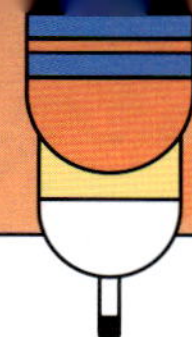

영작 기본 훈련

STEP 1 수동태 문장 **비교하기**

1 allow

a 이곳에는 반려동물이 **허용된다.**
Pets __________ __________ here.

b 이곳에는 반려동물이 **허용되지 않는다.**
Pets __________ __________ __________ here.

c 이곳에는 반려동물이 **허용되나요?**
__________ pets __________ here?

2 interest

a 그는 과학에 **관심이 있다.**
He __________ __________ __________ science.

b 그는 과학에 **관심이 있니?**
__________ he __________ __________ science?

c 그는 과학에 **관심이 있을지도 모른다.**
He __________ __________ __________ __________ science.

3 build

a 그 도서관은 2015년에 **지어졌니?**
__________ the library __________ in 2015?

b 그 도서관은 2015년에 **지어지지 않았다.**
The library __________ __________ __________ in 2015.

c 그 도서관은 **언제 지어졌니?**
__________ __________ the library __________?

4 crowd

a 그 거리는 관광객들로 **붐볐다.**
The street __________ __________ __________ tourists.

b 그 거리는 관광객들로 **붐볐니?**
__________ the street __________ __________ tourists?

c 그 거리는 관광객들로 **붐비지 않았다.**
The street __________ __________ __________ __________ tourists.

5 speak

a 그 지역에서는 프랑스어가 **말해진다.**
French __________ __________ in the area.

b 그 지역에서는 프랑스어가 **말해지니?**
__________ French __________ in the area?

c 그 지역에서는 프랑스어가 **말해지지 않는다.**
French __________ __________ __________ in the area.

6 write

a 그 에세이는 영어로 **작성되었다.**
The essay __________ __________ in English.

b 그 에세이는 영어로 **작성되었니?**
__________ the essay __________ in English?

c 그 에세이는 영어로 **작성되어야 한다.**
The essay __________ __________ __________ in English.

STEP 2 영작 완성하기

| 보기 | watch | fill | satisfy | invite | guess |

1 그녀는 그 결혼식에 초대받지 못했다.

→ She ___________ ___________ ___________ to the wedding.

2 Hill 씨 부부는 그들의 호텔 방에 만족했다.

→ Mr. and Mrs. Hill ___________ ___________ ___________ their hotel room.

3 그 쇼는 많은 사람들에 의해 시청되니?

→ ___________ the show ___________ ___________ many people?

4 그의 입은 케이크로 가득 차 있다.

→ His mouth ___________ ___________ ___________ cake.

5 취약한 비밀번호는 쉽게 추측될 수 있다.

→ Weak passwords ___________ ___________ easily ___________.

STEP 3 배열 영작하기

1 이 가게에서는 생화는 판매되지 않는다. not, are, fresh flowers, sold

→ ____ at this store.

2 아메리카 대륙은 Columbus에 의해 발견되었니? Columbus, discovered, America, was, by

→ ____

3 그 재킷은 손으로 세탁될 수 있다. by hand, can, the jacket, washed, be

→ ____

4 나는 너의 성공에 기쁘다. I, with, am, success, pleased, your

→ ____

5 그 약은 냉장고에 보관되어야 한다. be, the medicine, kept, must, in the refrigerator

→ ____

집중 훈련 **1** 틀린 부분 고치기

어법상 **틀린** 부분을 찾아 바르게 고치시오.

집중 훈련 **2** 영작 완성하기

주어진 말을 활용하여 문장을 완성하시오.

01 The gift was wrapped by she.
그 선물은 그녀에 의해 포장되었다.

____________ → ____________

02 Are you worried by the presentation?
너는 발표에 대해 걱정하니?

____________ → ____________

03 A surprise party will held for Jamie.
Jamie를 위해 깜짝 파티가 열릴 것이다.

____________ → ____________

04 Cell phones are allowed not in class.
수업 중에는 휴대 전화가 허용되지 않는다.

____________ → ____________

05 The sea can see from that room.
그 방에서 바다가 보일 수 있다.

____________ → ____________

06 Did the reviews written in English?
그 후기들은 영어로 작성되었니?

____________ → ____________

07 I am not interested by fashion.
나는 패션에 관심이 없다.

____________ → ____________

08 그 주차장은 차들로 가득 차 있다. (fill)

→ The parking lot ________________ cars.

09 그 건물은 Fox 씨에 의해 설계되지 않았다. (design)

→ The building ________________
Mr. Fox.

10 그녀는 작곡가로 알려져 있다. (know)

→ She ________________ a composer.

11 그 상자들은 어제 다른 곳으로 옮겨졌니?
(the boxes, move)

→ ________________ to another
place yesterday?

12 오늘 공항은 여행객들로 붐빌지도 모른다.
(may, crowd)

→ The airport ________________
travelers today.

13 우리는 그녀의 무례한 행동에 놀라지 않았다. (surprise)

→ We ________________ her rude
behavior.

14 이 물품들은 벼룩시장에서 팔릴 것이다. (will, sell)

→ These items ________________ at the
flea market.

주어진 말을 활용하여 영작하시오.

우리말과 의미가 같도록 〈조건〉에 맞게 영작하시오.

15 그녀의 소설은 작년에 출판되지 않았다.
(novel, publish, last year)

→ _______________________________________

16 그 소식은 보도되어야 한다. (the news, report)

→ _______________________________________

17 Colin은 벌을 무서워한다. (scare, bees)

→ _______________________________________

18 그 자전거는 그에 의해 고장 났니? (the bike, break)

→ _______________________________________

19 그 소파는 흰색 천으로 덮여 있다.
(sofa, a white cloth, cover)

→ _______________________________________

20
> **A** 그 카메라는 수리되었니? (the camera, fix)
> **B** Yes, it was.

→ _______________________________________

21
> **A** 우리의 수학여행은 취소될 거야.
> (school trip, cancel)
> **B** Oh, no. Why?

→ _______________________________________

22 그 노래가 그들에 의해 불렸다.

> 조건 **1** 주어진 말을 사용할 것
> (the song, sing)
> **2** 필요시 형태를 변형할 것
> **3** 6단어의 문장으로 쓸 것

→ _______________________________________

23 그가 내 선물에 기뻐했니?

> 조건 **1** 주어진 말을 활용할 것
> (please, my gift)
> **2** be동사를 사용할 것
> **3** 6단어의 문장으로 쓸 것

→ _______________________________________

24 그 새 영화는 내일 개봉될 것이다.

> 조건 **1** 괄호 안에 주어진 말을 활용할 것
> (movie, release)
> **2** 조동사 will을 사용할 것
> **3** 모두 7단어로 쓸 것

→ _______________________________________

25 그녀는 그녀의 성적에 만족할지도 모른다.

> 조건 **1** may, satisfy, her grade를 모두 사용할 것
> **2** 필요시 형태를 변형할 것
> **3** 7단어의 문장으로 쓸 것

→ _______________________________________

서술형 1 (4점)

우리말과 의미가 같도록 주어진 말을 활용하여 영작하시오.

> 영어는 많은 나라들에서 말해진다.
> (speak, in many countries)

→ ______________________________

서술형 2 (9점, 각 3점)

우리말과 의미가 같도록 〈보기〉에서 알맞은 말을 골라 문장을 완성하시오.

보기	call	grow	use

(1) 미국에서는 쌀이 재배되니?

→ ___________ rice ___________ in the United States?

(2) 이 동전들은 요즘에는 사용되지 않는다.

→ These coins ___________________ these days.

(3) 내 이름이 선생님에 의해 불렸다.

→ My name ___________________ the teacher.

서술형 3 NEW (4점, 각 2점)

그림을 보고, 〈조건〉에 맞게 영작하시오.

조건 1 과거시제를 사용하시오.
　　 2 주어진 말을 각 문장에서 한 번씩 사용하시오.
　　　 (my grandfather, this tree, plant)

(1) 능동태: ______________________________

(2) 수동태: ______________________________

서술형 4 (5점)

우리말과 의미가 같도록 〈조건〉에 맞게 영작하시오.

> 예약은 온라인으로 이루어질 수 있다.

조건 1 수동태 문장으로 쓰시오.
　　 2 알맞은 조동사를 사용하시오.
　　 3 주어진 말을 모두 활용해 5단어로 쓰시오.
　　　 (reservations, make, online)

→ ______________________________

서술형 5 (4점)

다음 문장을 수동태로 바꿔 쓰고, 생략 가능한 부분에 괄호를 하시오.

> Someone destroyed the ancient buildings 2,000 years ago.
> → The ancient buildings ___________________
> ___________________________________.

서술형 6 (4점)

①~⑤ 중 어법상 틀린 부분을 찾아 바르게 고쳐 쓰시오.

> *The Starry Night* is a very famous painting. It ①was painted by Vincent van Gogh. He ②was painted it from the window of his room. It ③was painted in 1889, but it is still loved ④by many people today. It ⑤is now displayed at a museum in New York City.

______________________ → ______________________

문장의 구조

A 수여동사는 '~에게 …을 (해) 주다'라는 의미를 나타내며, 「주어＋수여동사＋간접목적어＋직접목적어」의 형태로 쓴다.

Sally **sent** them a Christmas card.   Sally는 그들에게 크리스마스 카드를 보냈다.
간접목적어(~에게)   직접목적어(…을)

B 「주어＋수여동사＋직접목적어＋전치사＋간접목적어」의 형태로 바꿔 쓸 수 있다.

Frank	**gave**	me		a movie ticket	.
		간접목적어		직접목적어	

Frank	**gave**	a movie ticket	to	me	.
		직접목적어	전치사	간접목적어	

주의 직접목적어가 대명사일 때는 「주어＋수여동사＋직접목적어＋전치사＋간접목적어」의 형태로만 쓴다.

Frank gave **it** to me. (○)   Frank gave me <u>it</u>. (×)

TIP 동사에 따라 간접목적어 앞에 오는 전치사가 달라진다.

to	give, send, bring, pass, lend, show, teach, tell 등	Please **pass** *me* the sugar. → Please **pass** the sugar **to** *me*.
for	make, buy, get, cook 등	My uncle **made** *me* a tree house. → My uncle **made** a tree house **for** *me*.
of	ask 등	She **asked** *me* a favor. → She **asked** a favor **of** *me*.

1 수여동사가 있는 문장 구조 익히기

		주어	수여동사	간접목적어	직접목적어
e.g.	나는 <u>그에게</u> <u>내 주소를</u> 말해 주었다.	I	told	<u>him</u>	<u>my address</u> .
1	그녀의 팬들은 <u>그녀에게</u> <u>편지들을</u> 보냈다.	Her fans	sent	________	________ .
2	나의 개는 <u>나에게</u> <u>내 전화기를</u> 가져다주었다.	My dog	brought	________	________ .
3	김 선생님은 <u>우리에게</u> <u>수학을</u> 가르치신다.	Mr. Kim	teaches	________	________ .
4	그들은 <u>Jack에게</u> <u>새 신발을</u> 사 주었다.	They	bought	________	________ .
5	나는 <u>내 가족에게</u> <u>저녁 식사를</u> 요리해 준다.	I	cook	________	________ .

2 수여동사가 있는 문장 **형태 익히기**

1 나는 그에게 장갑을 만들어 주었다. (gloves)

→ I made ___________ ___________ ___________.

2 저에게 여권을 보여 주세요. (your passport)

→ Please show ___________ ___________ ___________.

3 그는 우리에게 재미있는 이야기를 해 주었다. (interesting stories)

→ He told ___________ ___________ ___________.

4 그 기자는 그녀에게 많은 질문을 했다. (many questions)

→ The reporter asked ___________ ___________ ___________.

5 그 아이들의 부모는 그들에게 새 책가방을 사 주었다. (new backpacks)

→ The kids' parents bought ___________ ___________ ___________ ___________.

3 수여동사가 있는 문장 **바꿔 쓰기**

e.g.
Bob sent me text messages.

→ Bob *sent text messages to me* ___________.

1 Nancy got her grandfather some tea.

→ Nancy ___________.

2 My aunt gave me a nice hat.

→ My aunt ___________.

3 Steve passed the water bottle to me.

→ Steve ___________.

4 I will lend my textbook to you.

→ I will ___________.

5 Can you bring me a blanket?

→ Can you ___________?

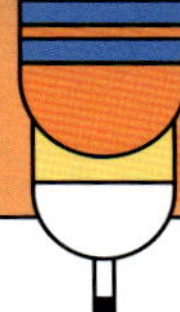

영작 기본 훈련

STEP 1 수여동사가 있는 문장 **비교하기**

e.g. **ⓐ** 나는 편지를 썼다.	I wrote a letter.
ⓑ 나는 **너에게** 편지를 썼다.	I ___wrote___ ___you___ ___a___ ___letter___ .
	I ___wrote___ ___a___ ___letter___ ___to___ you.

1
ⓐ 그들은 불고기를 요리했다.
They cooked bulgogi.

ⓑ 그들은 **우리에게** 불고기를 요리해 줬다.
They ________ ________ ________.
They ________ ________ ________ us.

2
ⓐ Green 선생님은 과학을 가르치신다.
Ms. Green teaches science.

ⓑ Green 선생님은 **그들에게** 과학을 가르치신다.
Ms. Green ________ ________ ________.
Ms. Green ________ ________ ________ them.

3
ⓐ 그녀는 손목시계를 샀다.
She bought a watch.

ⓑ 그녀는 **그에게** 손목시계를 사 주었다.
She ________ ________ ________ ________.
She ________ ________ ________ ________ him.

4
ⓐ 우리는 부탁 하나를 했다.
We asked a favor.

ⓑ 우리는 **그녀에게** 부탁 하나를 했다.
We ________ ________ ________.
We ________ ________ ________ ________ her.

5
ⓐ 그는 오렌지 주스를 만들었다.
He made orange juice.

ⓑ 그는 **우리에게** 오렌지 주스를 만들어 주었다.
He ________ ________ ________ ________.
He ________ ________ ________ ________ us.

STEP **2** 영작 **완성하기**

> 그는 나에게 기회를 주었다. (give)
>
> → He ___*gave*___ me ___*a*___ ___*chance*___ .

1 David는 Sally에게 그의 공책을 빌려주었다. (lend)

→ David ___________ Sally ___________ ___________ .

2 내가 너에게 물을 좀 가져다줄게. (get)

→ I will ___________ ___________ ___________ ___________ you.

3 나에게 소금을 건네줄래? (pass)

→ Can you ___________ ___________ ___________ ___________ ?

4 Sarah는 그녀의 반 친구들에게 가족사진을 보여 주었다. (show)

→ Sarah ___________ her family photo ___________ ___________ ___________ .

┤ 보기 ├
some water
the salt
~~a chance~~
his notebook
her classmates

STEP **3** 배열 **영작하기**

1 Jack은 그의 여자 친구에게 스파게티를 요리해 주었다. for, spaghetti, cooked, his girlfriend

→ Jack ____ .

2 그는 우리에게 중국어 단어 몇 개를 가르쳐 주었다. taught, he, some Chinese words, us

→ ____

3 나의 새 이웃이 나에게 부탁을 했다. a favor, of, asked, me, my new neighbor

→ ____

4 나는 부모님께 티셔츠를 사 드렸다. my parents, I, T-shirts, for, bought

→ ____

5 그 점원은 그녀에게 파란색 재킷을 가져다주었다. a blue jacket, brought, her, the clerk

→ ____

A 목적격 보어는 목적어를 보충 설명하는 말로, 동사에 따라 명사, 형용사, to부정사 등을 쓴다.

The song **made** <u>the singer</u> <u>famous</u>.   그 노래는 <u>그 가수를</u> <u>유명하게</u> 만들었다.
            목적어   목적격 보어

B 목적격 보어로 명사나 형용사를 쓰는 동사에는 make, call, name, keep, find 등이 있다.

주어	동사	목적어	목적격 보어	
People	**call**	her	"bookworm."	사람들은 <u>그녀를</u> '책벌레'라고 부른다.
They	**named**	their son	Liam.	그들은 <u>그들의 아들을</u> Liam이라고 이름 지었다.
The coat	**kept**	me	warm.	그 외투는 <u>나를</u> <u>따뜻하게</u> 유지해 주었다.
I	**found**	it	interesting.	나는 <u>그것이</u> <u>재미있다고</u> 생각했다.

주의 목적격 보어 자리에 오는 형용사가 '~하게'라고 해석된다고 해서 부사를 쓰지 않도록 주의한다.

She makes us **happy**. (○)   She makes us <u>happily</u>. (×)

1 목적격 보어가 있는 문장 **구조 익히기**

		주어	동사	목적어	목적격 보어
e.g.	나는 <u>그 이야기가</u> <u>웃기다고</u> 생각했다.	I	found	the story	funny .
1	아빠는 <u>내 남동생을</u> <u>Picasso라고</u> 부른다.	Dad	calls	__________	__________ .
2	<u>그 노래는</u> <u>나를</u> <u>행복하게</u> 했다.	The song	made	__________	__________ .
3	그 바람이 <u>우리를</u> <u>시원하게</u> 유지해 주었다.	The wind	kept	__________	__________ .
4	우리는 <u>우리 개를</u> <u>Bear라고</u> 이름 지었다.	We	named	__________	__________ .

2 형용사 보어 **형태 익히기**

1 그의 실수는 나를 화나게 만들었다. (make)   → His mistake __________ me __________.

2 우리는 방을 깨끗하게 유지해야 한다. (keep)   → We have to __________ our room __________.

3 나는 그 영화가 슬프다고 생각했다. (find)   → I __________ the movie __________.

 3 목적격 보어가 있는 문장 2 | to부정사

목적격 보어로 to부정사를 쓰는 동사에는 want, ask, tell, allow, expect, advise, order 등이 있다.

주어	동사	목적어	목적격 보어
He	**allowed**	us	to play games.
We	**expect**	you	to pass the test.
The doctor	**advised**	me	to exercise regularly.

그는 우리가 게임을 하는 것을 허락했다.
우리는 네가 시험에 합격하기를 기대한다.
의사는 나에게 규칙적으로 운동하라고 권고했다.

--------> 목적어는 의미상으로 to부정사가 나타내는 행위의 주체이다.

1 to부정사 보어 의미 익히기

e.g. Anna wants me to help her. → Anna는 ___내가 그녀를 도와주기를___ 원한다.

1 They expect him to become a pianist. → 그들은 _________________________ 기대한다.

2 I asked her to turn off the light. → 나는 _________________________ 부탁했다.

3 Kate allowed me to use her phone. → Kate는 _________________________ 허락했다.

4 Sam told them to leave his room. → Sam은 _________________________ 말했다.

5 She advised us to check the weather. → 그녀는 _________________________ 조언했다.

2 to부정사 보어 형태 적용하기

1 선생님은 우리가 열심히 공부하기를 기대하신다. (study)

→ The teacher expects __________ __________ __________ hard.

2 코치는 그의 선수들에게 휴식을 취하라고 말했다. (his players, take)

→ The coach told __________ __________ __________ __________ a break.

3 나는 어머니에게 나를 학교에 차로 데려다 달라고 부탁했다. (my mother, drive)

→ I asked __________ __________ __________ __________ me to school.

4 그의 부모님은 그가 밤늦게 외출하는 것을 허락하지 않으신다. (go out)

→ His parents don't allow __________ __________ __________ __________ late at night.

5 경찰관은 그들에게 차를 세우라고 명령했다. (stop)

→ The police officer ordered __________ __________ __________ the car.

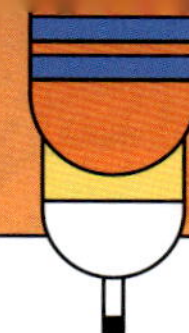

영작 기본 훈련

STEP 1 목적격 보어가 있는 문장으로 **확장하기**

1
ⓐ 그녀는 천사였다.　　She was an angel.

ⓑ 그는 **그녀를 천사라고** 불렀다.　　He called ＿＿＿＿＿ ＿＿＿＿＿ ＿＿＿＿＿.

2
ⓐ 그는 친절했다.　　He was friendly.

ⓑ 우리는 **그가 친절하다고** 생각했다.　　We found ＿＿＿＿＿ ＿＿＿＿＿.

3
ⓐ 창문이 열려 있다.　　The window is open.

ⓑ 나는 **창문을 열어** 두고 싶다.　　I want to keep ＿＿＿＿＿ ＿＿＿＿＿ ＿＿＿＿＿.

4
ⓐ 그 책은 베스트셀러이다.　　The book is a bestseller.

ⓑ 그 기사는 **그 책을 베스트셀러로** 만들었다.　　The article made ＿＿＿＿＿ ＿＿＿＿＿ ＿＿＿＿＿ ＿＿＿＿＿.

5
ⓐ 우리는 일어섰다.　　We stood up.

ⓑ 그는 **우리에게 일어서라고** 명령했다.　　He ordered ＿＿＿＿＿ ＿＿＿＿＿ ＿＿＿＿＿ ＿＿＿＿＿.

6
ⓐ 나는 그의 사진을 찍었다.　　I took his picture.

ⓑ 그는 **내가 그의 사진을 찍는 것을** 허락했다.　　He allowed ＿＿＿＿＿ ＿＿＿＿＿ ＿＿＿＿＿ his picture.

7
ⓐ 그들은 조용했다.　　They were quiet.

ⓑ 나는 **그들에게 조용히 해 달라고** 부탁했다.　　I asked ＿＿＿＿＿ ＿＿＿＿＿ ＿＿＿＿＿ ＿＿＿＿＿.

8
ⓐ 나는 일찍 집에 도착했다.　　I got home early.

ⓑ 엄마는 **내가 일찍 집에 도착할 거라고** 기대하셨다.　　My mom expected ＿＿＿＿＿ ＿＿＿＿＿ ＿＿＿＿＿ home early.

STEP **2** 영작 완성하기

1 규칙적인 운동은 우리를 건강하게 유지시켜 줄 수 있다. (keep, healthy)

→ Regular exercise can ___________ ___________ __________.

2 나의 친구들은 나를 Casper라고 부른다. (call, Casper)

→ My friends ___________ ___________ __________.

3 그 트레이너는 그에게 체중을 줄이라고 말했다. (tell, lose)

→ The trainer ___________ ___________ ___________ ___________ weight.

4 Laura는 그들이 침대를 옮겨 주기를 원했다. (want, move)

→ Laura __________ ___________ __________ __________ the bed.

5 나의 부모님은 내가 그 콘서트에 가는 것을 허락하셨다. (allow, go)

→ My parents ___________ __________ __________ _________ to the concert.

STEP **3** 배열 영작하기

1 드라이아이스는 아이스크림을 차갑게 유지시켜 줄 것이다. cold, the ice cream, will, keep

→ The dry ice ____.

2 그는 나에게 그의 책을 돌려 달라고 요청했다. he, to, asked, his book, me, return

→ ____

3 우리는 세상을 더 나은 곳으로 만들 수 있다. the world, make, we, a better place, can

→ ____

4 그녀는 Tim에게 최선을 다하라고 조언했다. Tim, she, do, advised, his best, to

→ ____

5 나는 네가 여기에 올 거라고 예상하지 못했다. you, come here, to, expect, I, didn't

→ ____

지각동사(see, hear, smell, feel 등)는 '~가 …하는 것을 보다/듣다/냄새 맡다/느끼다'라는 의미를 나타내며, 목적격 보어로 동사원형을 쓴다.

주어	동사	목적어	목적격 보어	
We	**saw**	him	swim.	우리는 <u>그가</u> <u>수영하는 것을</u> 보았다.
I	**heard**	you	cry.	나는 <u>네가</u> <u>우는 것을</u> 들었다.
People	**felt**	the building	shake.	사람들은 <u>건물이</u> <u>흔들리는 것을</u> 느꼈다.

cf. 목적어의 동작이 진행 중임을 강조할 때는 지각동사의 목적격 보어로 동사원형 대신 현재분사를 쓰기도 한다.
  We **saw** him **swimming** in the lake. 　우리는 그가 호수에서 <u>수영하고 있는 것을</u> 보았다.

1 지각동사의 목적격 보어 형태 익히기

e.g.	sing	그녀가 노래하는 것을 듣다	hear _____*her*_____ _____*sing(singing)*_____	
1	**dance**	그가 춤추는 것을 보다	watch __________ ______________	
2	**blow**	바람이 부는 것을 느끼다	feel the __________ ______________	
3	**fight**	그들이 싸우는 것을 보다	see __________ ______________	
4	**talk**	우리가 말하는 것을 듣다	listen to __________ ______________	

2 지각동사가 있는 문장 형태 적용하기

1 그녀는 무언가가 타고 있는 냄새를 맡았다.

→ She __________ something __________.

2 그들은 그녀가 빨간불에 멈춰 서는 것을 보았다.

→ They __________ her __________ at the red light.

3 나는 나의 고양이가 내 손을 핥고 있는 것을 느꼈다.

→ I __________ my cat __________ my hand.

4 Chris는 누군가가 계단을 걸어 올라가는 소리를 들었다.

→ Chris __________ someone __________ up the stairs.

보기
stop
licking
burning
walk

 5 목적격 보어가 있는 문장 4 | 사역동사

사역동사(make, have, let 등)는 '~가 …하게 하다'의 의미를 나타내며, 목적격 보어로 동사원형을 쓴다.

주어	동사	목적어	목적격 보어	
The joke	**made**	them	laugh.	그 농담은 그들을 웃게 했다.
They	**had**	us	stand in line.	그들은 우리가 줄을 서게 했다.
My sister	**let**	me	wear her clothes.	언니는 내가 그녀의 옷을 입게 해 주었다.

cf. help는 목적격 보어로 동사원형과 to부정사 둘 다 쓸 수 있다.
I **helped** her **wash**(**to wash**) the dishes.   나는 그녀가 설거지하는 것을 도왔다.

➕ 사역동사 make, have, let은 강제성의 정도에 차이가 있다.
make(~하게 시키다) > **have**(~하게 하다) > **let**(~하게 허락하다(두다))

1 사역동사의 목적격 보어 형태 익히기

1 study 우리가 공부하게 하다 → make _____________ _____________

2 enter 그녀를 들어오게 하다 → have _____________ _____________

3 sleep 내가 자도록 두다 → let _____________ _____________

4 work 그들이 일하는 것을 돕다 → help _____________ _____________

2 사역동사가 있는 문장 형태 적용하기

보기	grow sit down wait outside use her laptop

1 그는 모든 학생을 앉게 했다. (have)

→ He _____________ every student _____________________.

2 Kate는 내가 그녀의 노트북을 사용하도록 허락했다. (let)

→ Kate _____________ me _____________________.

3 물은 식물이 자라는 것을 돕는다. (help)

→ Water _____________ plants _____________________.

4 Alex는 그의 개를 밖에서 기다리게 했다. (make)

→ Alex _____________ his dog _____________________.

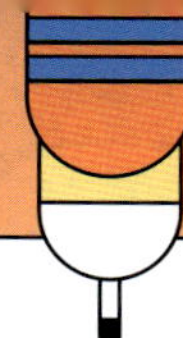

영작 기본 훈련

STEP 1 목적격 보어가 있는 문장으로 **확장하기**

1
ⓐ 그녀는 테니스를 쳤다.　　She played tennis.

ⓑ 우리는 **그녀가 테니스 치는 것을** 보았다.　　We ＿＿＿＿ ＿＿＿＿ ＿＿＿＿ tennis.

2
ⓐ 벨이 울렸다.　　The bell rang.

ⓑ 그녀는 **벨이 울리는 것을** 들었다.　　She ＿＿＿＿ ＿＿＿＿ ＿＿＿＿ ＿＿＿＿.

3
ⓐ 빗방울들이 내 머리 위로 떨어졌다.　　Raindrops fell on my head.

ⓑ 나는 **빗방울들이 내 머리 위로 떨어지는 것을** 느꼈다.　　I ＿＿＿＿ ＿＿＿＿ ＿＿＿＿ on my head.

4
ⓐ 무언가가 타고 있었다.　　Something was burning.

ⓑ 나는 **무언가가 타고 있는 냄새를** 맡았다.　　I ＿＿＿＿ ＿＿＿＿ ＿＿＿＿.

5
ⓐ 우리는 게임을 했다.　　We played games.

ⓑ 나의 부모님은 **우리가 게임을 하게** 허락했다.　　My parents ＿＿＿＿ ＿＿＿＿ ＿＿＿＿ games.

6
ⓐ 그들은 피아노를 옮겼다.　　They moved the piano.

ⓑ 그녀는 **그들이 피아노를 옮기게** 했다.　　She ＿＿＿＿ ＿＿＿＿ ＿＿＿＿ the piano.

7
ⓐ Kate는 반지를 찾았다.　　Kate found her ring.

ⓑ 그는 **Kate가 반지를 찾는 것을** 도왔다.　　He ＿＿＿＿ ＿＿＿＿ ＿＿＿＿ her ring.

8
ⓐ 그는 내 자전거를 수리했다.　　He fixed my bike.

ⓑ 나는 **그가 내 자전거를 수리하게** 했다.　　I ＿＿＿＿ ＿＿＿＿ ＿＿＿＿ my bike.

STEP **2** 영작 완성하기

1 아빠는 우리가 저녁 식사 후에 개를 산책시키도록 했다. (have, walk our dog)

→ Dad ___________ ___________ ___________ ___________ ___________ after dinner.

2 나는 무언가가 내 뒤에서 움직이는 것을 느꼈다. (feel, move)

→ I ___________ ___________ ___________ behind me.

3 그녀는 자신의 고양이가 부엌에 들어오지 못하게 했다. (let, enter)

→ She didn't ___________ ___________ ___________ ___________ the kitchen.

4 나는 Helen이 길을 따라 걸어가는 것을 보았다. (see, walk)

→ I ___________ ___________ ___________ along the street.

5 나의 선생님은 내가 그 프로젝트를 수행하게 했다. (make, do)

→ My teacher ___________ ___________ ___________ the project.

STEP **3** 배열 영작하기

1 Emily는 그가 영화를 고르도록 했다.   the movie, let, choose, him

→ Emily ____ .

2 자명종이 그녀를 일찍 일어나게 했다.   made, wake up, her, early

→ The alarm ____ .

3 우리는 별들이 하늘에서 빛나는 것을 보았다.   saw, in the sky, shining, we, the stars

→ ____

4 나는 누군가가 나를 따라오고 있는 소리를 들었다.   I, someone, me, heard, following

→ ____

5 그는 우리가 그 문제를 푸는 것을 도와주었다.   to, he, solve, the problem, us, helped

→ ____

집중 훈련 **1** 틀린 부분 고치기
어법상 틀린 부분을 찾아 바르게 고치시오.

집중 훈련 **2** 영작 완성하기
주어진 말을 활용하여 문장을 완성하시오.

01 My uncle gave to me a skateboard.
나의 삼촌은 내게 스케이트보드를 주셨다.

_______________ → _______________

02 Mr. Lee told us write a book report.
이 선생님은 우리에게 독후감을 쓰라고 말씀하셨다.

_______________ → _______________

03 I made delicious cookies to my friends.
나는 친구들에게 맛있는 쿠키를 만들어 주었다.

_______________ → _______________

04 You should keep the food freshly.
너는 그 음식을 신선하게 유지해야 한다.

_______________ → _______________

05 The teacher had the students turned off their cell phones.
그 선생님은 학생들이 휴대 전화를 끄도록 했다.

_______________ → _______________

06 He helped us setting up the tent.
그는 우리가 텐트를 치는 것을 도와주었다.

_______________ → _______________

07 I heard him laughed loudly.
나는 그가 큰 소리로 웃는 것을 들었다.

_______________ → _______________

08 Harry는 그들이 그 동아리에 가입하기를 원했다.
(join, want)

→ Harry _______________________ the club.

09 나는 Eric에게 초콜릿을 사 주었다. (chocolate, buy)

→ I _______________________ Eric.

10 좋은 날씨는 우리를 행복하게 만들었다. (happy, make)

→ The nice weather _______________________.

11 그 남자는 나에게 시청으로 가는 길을 알려 주었다.
(the way, show)

→ The man _______________________ to City Hall.

12 그녀의 팬들은 그녀를 공주라고 부른다.
(a princess, call)

→ Her fans _______________________.

13 Tom은 그의 남동생이 새로운 비디오 게임을 하도록 허락했다. (play, let)

→ Tom _______________________ his new video game.

14 그는 나에게 볼륨을 줄여 달라고 부탁했다.
(turn down, ask)

→ He _______________________ the volume.

집중 훈련 3 통문장 영작하기

주어진 말을 활용하여 영작하시오.

15 Amy는 그녀의 그림을 '행복'이라고 이름 지었다.
(*Happiness*, painting)

→ _______________________________________

16 Tony는 그의 심장이 빠르게 뛰는 것을 느꼈다.
(heart, beat fast)

→ _______________________________________

17 나의 언니는 내가 그녀의 전화기를 충전하게 했다.
(charge, have)

→ _______________________________________

18 그들은 숲을 깨끗하게 유지한다.
(the forest, clean, keep)

→ _______________________________________

19 그의 아빠는 그가 캠핑하러 가는 것을 허락했다.
(go camping, allow)

→ _______________________________________

20

| |
| A Did you send Sarah the present? |
| B Not yet. <u>나는 그것을 그녀에게 내일 보낼 거야.</u> |
| (will, send) |

→ _______________________________________

21

| |
| A Did you see Mark today? |
| B Yes, I did. |
| <u>나는 그가 공원에서 춤추는 것을 봤어.</u> |
| (dance, in the park) |

→ _______________________________________

집중 훈련 4 조건 영작하기

우리말과 의미가 같도록 〈조건〉에 맞게 영작하시오.

22 Ted는 그의 친구들에게 마술을 보여 주었다.

| 조건 1 주어진 말을 활용할 것 |
| (show, a magic trick) |
| 2 전치사를 포함할 것 |
| 3 8단어의 문장으로 쓸 것 |

→ _______________________________________

23 그녀는 그 영화가 흥미진진하고 생각했다.

| 조건 1 주어진 말을 활용할 것 |
| (find, exciting) |
| 2 5단어의 문장으로 쓸 것 |

→ _______________________________________

24 우리는 그가 상을 탈 것을 기대한다.

| 조건 1 괄호 안에 주어진 말을 활용할 것 |
| (expect, win the award) |
| 2 모두 7단어로 쓸 것 |

→ _______________________________________

25 Sarah는 한 남자가 밖에서 고함치는 소리를 들었다.

| 조건 1 hear, shout, outside를 사용할 것 |
| 2 필요시 형태를 변형할 것 |
| 3 6단어의 문장으로 쓸 것 |

→ _______________________________________

서술형 1 (3점)

우리말과 의미가 같도록 어법상 틀린 부분을 찾아 바르게 고쳐 쓰시오.

> 그녀는 내가 그녀에게 펜을 가져다주게 했다.
> → She had me to bring her a pen.

________________ → ________________

서술형 2 (4점)

그림을 보고, 주어진 말을 활용하여 문장을 완성하시오.

> Nicky ________________________ over the fence yesterday. (see, jump)

서술형 3 (6점, 각 3점)

다음 중 밑줄 친 부분이 어법상 틀린 문장 두 개를 찾아 기호를 쓰고, 바르게 고쳐 쓰시오.

> ⓐ My mom wants me to eat more.
> ⓑ They heard children to sing a song.
> ⓒ The news about the war made me sadly.
> ⓓ Tom advised me to get up early.

(1) ( ) → ________________

(2) ( ) → ________________

서술형 4 (4점)

우리말과 의미가 같도록 〈조건〉에 맞게 영작하시오.

> John은 내가 그의 자전거를 타는 것을 허락했다.

조건 1 주어진 말을 활용하시오.
        (allow, ride his bike)
      2 7단어의 문장으로 서술하시오.

→ ________________________________

서술형 5 NEW (4점)

다음 대화의 내용과 일치하도록 주어진 말을 사용하여 문장을 완성하시오.

> **Joe**   Mom, can I go to the movies with my friends this weekend?
> **Mom** Sure.

→ Joe's mom will ________________ to the movies with his friends. (let)

서술형 6 (9점, 각 3점)

다음 대화의 밑줄 친 우리말과 의미가 같도록 주어진 말을 사용하여 영작하시오. (전치사를 포함하는 문장으로 쓸 것)

> **Lisa** Did you have a nice weekend?
> **Ann**   I sure did! (1)나의 엄마는 내가 가장 좋아하는 음식을 나에게 요리해 주셨어. (my favorite food) (2)나의 아빠는 나에게 스마트폰을 사 주셨어. (a smartphone) (3)나의 언니는 나에게 헤드폰 한 쌍을 주었고. (a pair of headphones)
> **Lisa** Wow. Was it your birthday?
> **Ann**   Yes, it was.

(1) ________________________________

(2) ________________________________

(3) ________________________________

to부정사

to부정사의 명사적 용법 1

A to부정사는 명사처럼 주어, 목적어, 보어 역할을 하며, '~하는 것, ~하기'로 해석한다.

주어	**To read many books** is a good habit.
목적어	I want **to read many books**.
보어	My plan is **to read many books**.

→ 주어로 쓰인 to부정사(구)는 항상 단수 취급한다.

TIP to부정사의 부정은 to부정사 앞에 not이나 never를 써서 나타낸다.

We decided **not to leave**.   우리는 떠나지 않기로 결정했다.

B 「의문사+to부정사」는 주어, 목적어, 보어 역할을 하며 「의문사+주어+should+동사원형」으로 바꿔 쓸 수 있다.

| **what+to부정사** | 무엇을 ~할지 | **how+to부정사** | 어떻게 ~할지, ~하는 방법 |
| **where+to부정사** | 어디에(서)/어디로 ~할지 | **when+to부정사** | 언제 ~할지 |

I don't know **what to do**.

    (→ **what I should do**)

→ why는 「why+to부정사」 형태로 쓰지 않는다.
I don't know why to go there. (x)

1 명사적 용법 역할 익히기

1 롤러코스터는 재미있다. → Roller coasters are fun.

롤러코스터를 타는 것은 재미있다. (ride) →   is fun.

2 Judy는 소설을 좋아한다. → Judy likes novels .

Judy는 소설 읽는 것을 좋아한다. (read) → Judy likes   .

3 Sam의 꿈의 직업은 요리사이다. → Sam's dream job is a cook .

Sam의 꿈은 요리사가 되는 것이다. (be) → Sam's dream is   .

2 「의문사+to부정사」 형태 익히기

1 그는 나에게 언제 그 프로젝트를 시작할지 물었다. (start)

→ He asked me ___________ ___________ ___________ the project.

2 그들은 무엇을 사야 할지 몰랐다. (buy)

→ They didn't know ___________ ___________ ___________.

3 엄마는 나에게 어떻게 종이 비행기를 만드는지 가르쳐 주셨다. (make)

→ My mom taught me ___________ ___________ ___________ a paper airplane.

A to부정사(구)가 주어로 쓰일 때는 보통 주어 자리에 가주어 it을 쓰고 진주어인 to부정사(구)는 뒤로 보낸다.

To do your best is important.

→ **It** is important **to do your best**.
가주어   진주어

주의   가주어 it은 '그것'이라고 해석하지 않는다.

B to부정사의 동작을 행하는 주체를 나타내는 의미상 주어는 to부정사 앞에 「for/of+목적격」의 형태로 쓴다.

for+목적격	일반적인 형용사(easy, difficult, interesting, possible 등)	**It** is *difficult **for me** **to speak** in front of people. **It** is *dangerous **for you** **to climb** up the ladder.
of+목적격	사람의 성격·성향을 나타내는 형용사 (nice, kind, foolish, rude, wise 등)	**It** is *nice **of her** **to help** her sister. **It** was *kind **of him** **to show** us the way.

1 가주어 사용하여 문장 다시 쓰기

1 To send a thank-you card is nice.

→ ___________ is nice ___________ ___________ a thank-you card.

2 To respect others is important.

→ ___________ is important ___________ ___________ others.

3 To stay up late at night is not good.

→ ___________ is not good ___________ ___________ up late at night.

2 의미상 주어 형태 익히기

e.g. 네가 이곳에서 수영하는 것은 위험하다. (swim)

→ It is dangerous ___for___ ___you___ ___to___ ___swim___ here.

1 그를 믿다니 그들은 어리석었다. (trust)

→ It was foolish ___________ ___________ ___________ ___________ him.

2 우리가 그곳에 정시에 도착하는 것은 불가능하다. (get)

→ It is impossible ___________ ___________ ___________ ___________ there on time.

3 그녀가 그렇게 말한 것은 무례했다. (talk)

→ It was rude ___________ ___________ ___________ ___________ like that.

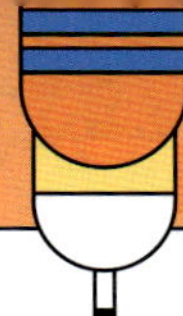

STEP 1 to부정사 문장 비교하기

A　명사적 용법의 역할 비교하기

1

ⓐ 그녀는 많은 꽃을 심는다.　　She plants many flowers.

ⓑ 그녀는 **많은 꽃을 심는 것을** 좋아한다.　　She likes ＿＿＿＿ ＿＿＿＿ ＿＿＿＿ ＿＿＿＿.

ⓒ 그녀의 목표는 **많은 꽃을 심는 것**이다.　　Her goal is ＿＿＿＿ ＿＿＿＿ ＿＿＿＿ ＿＿＿＿.

2

ⓐ 많은 외국인들은 한국어를 배운다.　　Many foreigners learn Korean.

ⓑ **한국어를 배우는 것은** 어렵다.　　＿＿＿＿ ＿＿＿＿ ＿＿＿＿ is difficult.

ⓒ 너는 **한국어를 배워야** 한다.　　You need ＿＿＿＿ ＿＿＿＿ ＿＿＿＿.

3

ⓐ Leo는 만화를 그린다.　　Leo draws cartoons.

ⓑ Leo는 **만화를 그리는 것을** 배웠다.　　Leo learned ＿＿＿＿ ＿＿＿＿ ＿＿＿＿.

ⓒ Leo의 직업은 **만화를 그리는 것**이다.　　Leo's job is ＿＿＿＿ ＿＿＿＿ ＿＿＿＿.

B　가주어와 의미상 주어가 있는 문장 비교하기

1

ⓐ **책을 쓰는 것**은 쉽다.　　＿＿＿＿ write books is easy.

ⓑ **책을 쓰는 것**은 쉽다.　　＿＿＿＿ is easy ＿＿＿＿ ＿＿＿＿ ＿＿＿＿.

ⓒ **그녀가 책을 쓰는 것**은 쉽다.　　It is easy ＿＿＿＿ ＿＿＿＿ ＿＿＿＿ ＿＿＿＿ books.

2

ⓐ **'please'라고 말하는 것**은 예의 바르다.　　＿＿＿＿ say please is polite.

ⓑ **'please'라고 말하는 것**은 예의 바르다.　　＿＿＿＿ is polite ＿＿＿＿ ＿＿＿＿ ＿＿＿＿.

ⓒ **네가 'please'라고 말하다니** 예의 발랐다.　　It was polite ＿＿＿＿ ＿＿＿＿ ＿＿＿＿ ＿＿＿＿ please.

3

ⓐ **돈을 기부하는 것**은 관대하다.　　＿＿＿＿ donate money is generous.

ⓑ **돈을 기부하는 것**은 관대하다.　　＿＿＿＿ is generous ＿＿＿＿ ＿＿＿＿ ＿＿＿＿.

ⓒ **그들이 돈을 기부하다니** 관대했다.　　It was generous ＿＿＿＿ ＿＿＿＿ ＿＿＿＿ ＿＿＿＿
money.

 4 to부정사의 부사적 용법

to부정사는 동사, 형용사, 또는 문장 전체를 수식하는 부사 역할을 한다.

목적	~하기 위해	They had to run **to catch** the bus. = They had to run **in order to catch** the bus.
감정의 원인	~해서, ~하게 되어서	I was happy **to see** you again.
판단의 근거	~하다니, ~하는 것을 보니	Tony must be kind **to help** his friends.
결과	(…해서) ~하다	The girl grew up **to be** a doctor.

목적의 의미를 강조할 때 쓴다.

TIP 감정의 원인을 나타내는 to부정사는 감정을 나타내는 형용사(glad, happy, sad, pleased, excited, upset 등) 뒤에 온다.

1 부사적 용법 의미 익히기

e.g. He lay on the bed to take a nap. → 그는 _낮잠을 자기 위해_ 침대에 누웠다.

1 We are sorry to hear the news. → 우리는 _______________________ 유감이다.

2 I was stupid to make a mistake. → _______________________ 나는 어리석었다.

3 I came here to meet you. → 나는 _______________________ 이곳에 왔다.

4 The child grew up to be a pilot. → 그 아이는 자라서 _______________________.

2 부사적 용법 형태 적용하기

| 보기 | spend | be | speak | repair |

1 5개 국어를 말하다니 Andy는 천재임이 틀림없다.

→ Andy must be a genius ___________ ___________ five languages.

2 나는 그들과 시간을 보내게 되어 정말 신났다.

→ I was really excited ___________ ___________ time with them.

3 나의 할아버지는 95세까지 사셨다.

→ My grandfather lived ___________ ___________ 95 years old.

4 아빠는 차를 고치기 위해 차고로 가셨다.

→ My dad went to the garage ___________ ___________ ___________ ___________ his car.

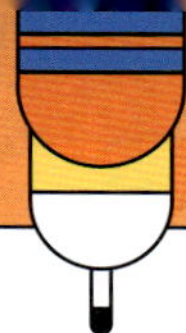

STEP 1 to부정사 의미 확장하기

A 형용사적 용법으로 확장하기

1
ⓐ 나는 무언가를 가지고 있다.　　　　I have something.

ⓑ 나는 너에게 **줄** 무언가를 가지고 있다.　　I have something __________ __________ you.

2
ⓐ 우리는 몇 가지 물건이 있다.　　　　We have a few things.

ⓑ 우리는 **사야 할** 몇 가지 물건이 있다.　　We have a few things __________ __________.

3
ⓐ 그는 종이가 필요하다.　　　　He needs paper.

ⓑ 그는 **쓸** 종이가 필요하다.　　He needs paper __________ __________ __________.

4
ⓐ 그녀는 노래 한 곡을 추천했다.　　She recommended a song.

ⓑ 그녀는 **들을** 노래 한 곡을 추천했다.　　She recommended a song __________ __________ __________.

B 부사적 용법으로 확장하기

1
ⓐ 그녀는 파리로 갔다.　　　　She went to Paris.

ⓑ 그녀는 미술을 **공부하기 위해** 파리로 갔다.　　She went to Paris __________ __________ art.

2
ⓐ 나는 기뻤다.　　　　I was glad.

ⓑ 나는 그 소식을 **들어서** 기뻤다.　　I was glad __________ __________ the news.

3
ⓐ 그는 운이 좋았다.　　　　He was lucky.

ⓑ **그녀를 만나다니** 그는 운이 좋았다.　　He was lucky __________ __________ __________.

4
ⓐ 그는 자랐다.　　　　He grew up.

ⓑ 그는 자라서 **가수가 되었다.**　　He grew up __________ __________ __________ __________.

STEP **2** 영작 완성하기

1 그 축제에는 즐길 활동들이 많이 있다. (enjoy, activities)

→ The festival has many ＿＿＿＿＿ ＿＿＿＿＿ ＿＿＿＿＿.

2 그 소문을 믿다니 너는 어리석다. (silly, believe)

→ You are ＿＿＿＿＿ ＿＿＿＿＿ ＿＿＿＿＿ the rumor.

3 우리는 그곳에 가기 위해 기차를 탔다. (get there)

→ We took the train ＿＿＿＿＿ ＿＿＿＿＿ ＿＿＿＿＿.

4 Amy는 같이 놀 친구들이 많이 있다. (play, friends)

→ Amy has a lot of ＿＿＿＿＿ ＿＿＿＿＿ ＿＿＿＿＿ ＿＿＿＿＿.

5 나는 그 경기를 이겨서 놀랐다. (win, surprised)

→ I was ＿＿＿＿＿ ＿＿＿＿＿ ＿＿＿＿＿ the game.

STEP **3** 배열 영작하기

1 나는 지금 당장 할 일이 아무것도 없다.   have, I, do, to, nothing

→ ＿＿＿＿＿＿＿＿＿＿＿＿＿＿＿＿＿＿ right now.

2 우리는 살 집을 샀다.   to, bought, we, in, a house, live

→ ＿＿＿＿＿＿＿＿＿＿＿＿＿＿＿＿＿＿

3 그 소녀는 자라서 위대한 과학자가 되었다.   a great scientist, grew up, the girl, be, to

→ ＿＿＿＿＿＿＿＿＿＿＿＿＿＿＿＿＿＿

4 나는 내 낮은 시험 점수를 보고 실망했다.   I, see, my low test score, was, to, disappointed

→ ＿＿＿＿＿＿＿＿＿＿＿＿＿＿＿＿＿＿

5 그는 그 그림들을 보기 위해 미술관에 갔다.   see, he, to, to, the museum, the paintings, went

→ ＿＿＿＿＿＿＿＿＿＿＿＿＿＿＿＿＿＿

too ~ to부정사 구문

「too+형용사/부사+to부정사」는 '…하기에 너무 ~한/하게' 또는 '너무 ~해서 …할 수 없는'이라는 의미로 「so+형용사/부사+that+주어+can't+동사원형」으로 바꿔 쓸 수 있다.

I am **too** shy **to speak** in public. 나는 사람들 앞에서 말하기에 너무 수줍음이 많다.

(→ I am **so** shy **that** I **can't speak** in public.) 나는 너무 수줍음이 많아서 사람들 앞에서 말할 수 없다.

We arrived **too** late **to take** the train.

(→ We arrived **so** late **that** we **couldn't take** the train.)

-----> 과거시제인 경우 couldn't를 쓴다.

TIP too는 '너무 (지나치게)'라는 의미가 있어 to부정사와 함께 쓰이면 문장 전체가 부정의 의미를 나타낸다.

1 too ~ to부정사 구문 형태 익히기

e.g.	tired, go	She was ____ too ____ tired ____ . 너무 피곤한 She was ____ too ____ tired ____ to ____ go ____ out. 외출하기에 너무 피곤한
1	lazy, work	He is ________________ . 너무 게으른 He is ____ ____ ____ ____ . 일하기에 너무 게으른
2	busy, cook	I'm ________________ tonight. 너무 바쁜 I'm ____ ____ ____ ____ tonight. 요리하기에 너무 바쁜

2 too ~ to부정사 구문 형태 적용하기

1 우리는 후식을 먹기에는 너무 배불렀다. (full, eat)

→ We were ____ ____ ____ ____ dessert.

2 내 여동생은 자동차를 운전하기에 너무 어리다. (young, drive)

→ My sister is ____ ____ ____ ____ a car.

3 Janet은 너무 졸려서 영화를 즐길 수 없었다. (sleepy, enjoy)

→ Janet was ____ ____ ____ ____ the movie.

4 그녀의 여행 가방은 들기에 너무 무거웠다. (heavy, lift)

→ Her suitcase was ____ ____ ____ ____ .

6 enough to부정사 구문

「형용사/부사＋enough＋to부정사」는 '…할 만큼 충분히 ~한/하게'라는 의미로 「so＋형용사/부사＋that＋주어＋can＋동사원형」으로 바꿔 쓸 수 있다.

He is fast **enough to win** the race.   그는 경주에서 우승할 만큼 충분히 빠르다.
(→ He is **so** fast **that** he **can win** the race.)   그는 매우 빨라서 경주에서 우승할 수 있다.

She was funny **enough to make** us laugh all the time.
(→ She was **so** funny **that** she **could make** us laugh all the time.)

------> 과거시제인 경우 could를 쓴다.

TIP 부사 enough는 too와 달리 형용사나 부사 뒤에 쓴다.
I was **too** *tired* to run a marathon.
I was *strong* **enough** to run a marathon.

1 enough to부정사 구문 형태 익히기

e.g. tall, reach	This ladder is ___tall___ ___enough___. 충분히 높은 This ladder is ___tall___ ___enough___ ___to___ ___reach___ the roof. 닿을 만큼 충분히 높은	
1 kind, help	He was ___________________. 충분히 친절한 He was _______________________________ them. 도울 만큼 충분히 친절한	
2 hard, build	She exercised ___________________. 충분히 열심히 She exercised _____________________________ muscle. 근육을 만들 만큼 충분히 열심히	

2 enough to부정사 구문 형태 적용하기

1 Green 씨는 그 집을 살 만큼 충분히 부유하다. (rich, buy)

→ Mr. Green is ___________ ___________ ___________ ___________ the house.

2 그 고양이는 쥐들을 잡을 만큼 충분히 조용하게 움직인다. (quietly, catch)

→ The cat moves ___________ ___________ ___________ ___________ mice.

3 Peter는 스스로 결정을 내릴 만큼 충분히 현명하다. (wise, make)

→ Peter is ___________ ___________ ___________ ___________ his own decisions.

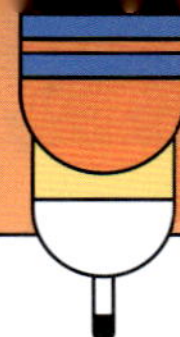

영작 기본 훈련

STEP **1** to부정사 구문 의미 **비교하기**

e.g.

travel / young / old

ⓐ 그녀는 혼자 **여행하기에** 너무 어리다.
→ She is ____too____ ____young____ ____to____ ____travel____ alone.

ⓑ 그녀는 혼자 **여행할 만큼 충분히 나이가 들었다.**
→ She is ____old____ ____enough____ ____to____ ____travel____ alone.

---

1 become / weak / strong

ⓐ 그는 레슬링 선수가 **되기에** 너무 약하다.
→ He is __________ __________ __________ a wrestler.

ⓑ 그는 레슬링 선수가 **될 만큼 충분히 힘이 세다.**
→ He is __________ __________ __________ a wrestler.

---

2 eat / cold / warm

ⓐ 야외에서 **식사하기에는** 너무 추웠다.
→ It was __________ __________ __________ __________ outside.

ⓑ 야외에서 **식사할 만큼 충분히 따뜻했다.**
→ It was __________ __________ __________ __________ outside.

---

3 catch / late / early

ⓐ 나는 **너무 늦게** 일어나서 버스를 **탈 수 없었다.**
→ I got up __________ __________ __________ the bus.

ⓑ 나는 버스를 **탈 만큼 충분히 일찍** 일어났다.
→ I got up __________ __________ __________ the bus.

---

4 carry / heavy / light

ⓐ 내 노트북 컴퓨터는 **가지고 다니기에** 너무 무겁다.
→ My laptop is __________ __________ __________ around.

ⓑ 내 노트북 컴퓨터는 **가지고 다닐 만큼 충분히 가볍다.**
→ My laptop is __________ __________ __________ around.

---

5 sing / shy / brave

ⓐ 나는 **너무 수줍어서** 무대 위에서 **노래를 부를 수 없었다.**
→ I was __________ __________ __________ on the stage.

ⓑ 나는 무대 위에서 **노래를 부를 만큼 충분히 용기 있었다.**
→ I was __________ __________ __________ on the stage.

STEP **2** 문장 전환하기

1 He is so smart that he can solve this crossword puzzle.

→ He is ___________ ___________ ___________ ___________ this crossword puzzle.

2 They worked so slowly that they couldn't finish the work on time.

→ They worked ___________ ___________ ___________ ___________ the work on time.

3 She feels good enough to go out.

→ She feels ___________ ___________ that ___________ ___________ ___________ out.

4 I'm so tired that I can't clean my bedroom.

→ I'm ___________ ___________ ___________ ___________ my bedroom.

5 Emma was too busy to eat lunch.

→ Emma was ___________ ___________ that ___________ ___________ ___________ lunch.

STEP **3** 배열 영작하기

1 Tim은 너무 배고파서 잠들 수 없었다. to, was, too, fall asleep, hungry

→ Tim ____ .

2 Vicky는 내 목숨을 구해 줄 만큼 충분히 수영을 잘했다. enough, swam, my life, save, to, well

→ Vicky ____ .

3 그녀는 배구 선수가 될 만큼 충분히 키가 크다. a volleyball player, is, to, tall, she, enough, be

→ ____

4 내 남동생은 이 영화를 보기에 너무 어리다. my brother, watch, young, is, to, this movie, too

→ ____

5 그 상자는 모든 책을 담을 만큼 충분히 크다. to, big, the box, all the books, is, hold, enough

→ ____

집중 훈련 1 틀린 부분 고치기
어법상 **틀린** 부분을 찾아 바르게 고치시오.

집중 훈련 2 영작 완성하기 (to부정사를 사용할 것)
주어진 말을 활용하여 문장을 완성하시오.

01
It was nice for you to drive her home.
그녀를 차로 집까지 바래다주다니 너는 착했다.

______________ → ______________

02
Amy is so sick to go to school.
Amy는 너무 아파서 학교에 갈 수 없다.

______________ → ______________

03
To have many things are not important in life.
많은 것을 가지는 것은 인생에서 중요하지 않다.

______________ → ______________

04
Jenny has a pencil to write.
Jenny는 쓸 연필 하나를 가지고 있다.

______________ → ______________

05
We were excited visit Busan.
우리는 부산을 방문하게 되어 신났다.

______________ → ______________

06
That is rude to talk loudly in a theater.
극장에서 큰 소리로 이야기하는 것은 무례하다.

______________ → ______________

07
We bought some flour in order make pizza.
우리는 피자를 만들기 위해 밀가루를 좀 샀다.

______________ → ______________

---

08 Sally는 하이킹을 하러 가기로 결심했다. (go, decide)

→ Sally ______________________ hiking.

09 그들은 그 공연을 보기에는 너무 늦게 도착했다.
(late, see)

→ They arrived ______________________
the show.

10 그가 그 강을 수영해서 건너는 것은 불가능하다. (swim)

→ It is impossible ______________________
across the river.

11 그 어린 소년은 자라서 소방관이 되었다.
(grow up, become)

→ The little boy ______________________
a firefighter.

12 나의 꿈은 하와이에서 사는 것이다. (live)

→ My dream ______________________ in Hawaii.

13 그의 거짓말을 믿다니 그들은 어리석었다.
(foolish, believe)

→ They were ______________________
his lies.

14 Sam은 내일까지 끝낼 보고서가 있다.
(a report, finish)

→ Sam has ______________________ by
tomorrow.

집중 훈련 3 통문장 영작하기 (to부정사를 사용할 것)
주어진 말을 활용하여 영작하시오.

15 언제 만날지에 대해 이야기해 보자. (let's, meet)

→ ___________________________

16 그는 그 롤러코스터를 타기에 너무 키가 작다.
(short, ride, the roller coaster)

→ ___________________________

17 우리는 다시는 싸우지 않기로 약속했다.
(promise, fight again)

→ ___________________________

18 그녀는 그 책장을 옮길 만큼 충분히 힘이 세다.
(strong, move the bookshelf)

→ ___________________________

19 나에게 기회를 주다니 그녀는 너그럽다.
(it, generous, give me a chance)

→ ___________________________

20
A Jane에게 전화하기 위해 내가 네 전화기를 써도
될까? (can, phone, call)
B Sure. Here it is.

→ ___________________________

21
A Why do you want to meet Tina?
B 나는 그녀에게 말할 것이 있어.
 (have, something, tell)

→ ___________________________

집중 훈련 4 조건 영작하기
우리말과 의미가 같도록 〈조건〉에 맞게 영작하시오.

22 그가 새로운 것들을 배우는 것은 쉽다.

조건 1 주어진 말을 사용할 것
 (easy, learn new things)
 2 it을 반드시 포함할 것
 3 9단어의 문장으로 쓸 것

→ ___________________________

23 나는 너무 긴장해서 나 자신을 소개할 수 없었다.

조건 1 주어진 말을 사용할 것
 (nervous, introduce myself)
 2 to부정사를 사용할 것
 3 7단어의 문장으로 쓸 것

→ ___________________________

24 그들은 그 경기에 져서 슬펐다.

조건 1 괄호 안에 주어진 말을 사용할 것
 (sad, lose the game)
 2 to부정사를 사용할 것
 3 7단어의 과거시제 문장으로 쓸 것

→ ___________________________

25 그녀는 자신의 가방을 어디에 두어야 할지 몰랐다.

조건 1 know, put, bag을 사용할 것
 2 의문사와 to부정사를 사용할 것
 3 총 8단어의 문장으로 쓸 것

→ ___________________________

서술형 1   (3점)

다음 두 문장의 의미가 같도록 빈칸에 알맞은 말을 쓰시오.

I saw Sarah again, so I was pleased.

→   I was ___________ ___________ ___________
    Sarah again.

서술형 2   (3점)

우리말과 의미가 같도록 주어진 말을 사용하여 문장을 완성하시오.

> 나의 고민을 들어 주다니 너는 무척 친절하구나.
> (kind, listen to)

→   It is very ___________ ___________ ___________
    ___________ ___________ ___________ my
    troubles.

서술형 3   (8점, 각 4점)

우리말과 의미가 같도록 〈조건〉에 맞게 영작하시오.

> (1) 그녀는 자라서 뛰어난 수영 선수가 되었다.

조건 1 주어진 말을 활용하시오.
         (grow up, an excellent swimmer)
      2 8단어의 문장으로 서술하시오.

→   ________________________________

> (2) 나를 도와줄 사람이 아무도 없었다.

조건 1 주어진 말을 활용하시오.
         (there, help, nobody)
      2 6단어의 문장으로 서술하시오.

→   ________________________________

서술형 4   (8점, 각 4점)

그림을 보고, 주어진 말을 사용하여 문장을 완성하시오.

(1)

→   Smartphones are ___________ ___________
    ___________ ___________ in one hand.
    (enough, small, hold)

(2)

→   Alex went to the store ___________ ___________
    ___________ ___________ ___________.
    (buy, something, drink)

서술형 5 NEW   (8점, 각 4점)

다음 글의 밑줄 친 우리말과 의미가 같도록 주어진 말을 사용하여 영작하시오. (to부정사를 포함하는 문장으로 쓸 것)

>   It is spring, so the weather is warm. Last
> Sunday, (1)나는 밖에서 놀게 되어서 신이 났다.
> (excited, play outside) I went to the river to
> swim. But I couldn't. (2)물은 수영하기에 너무
> 차가웠다. (the water, cold, swim in) I had to come
> home.

(1) ________________________________

(2) ________________________________

동명사

동명사는 「동사원형+-ing」의 형태로, 명사처럼 주어, 목적어, 보어 역할을 할 수 있으며, '~하는 것, ~하기'로 해석한다.

주어	**Swimming** is good for your health.
목적어	Ann *enjoys* **traveling** with her family. 〈동사의 목적어〉 I am interested *in* **writing** music. 〈전치사의 목적어〉
보어	His bad habit is **being** late for school.

> 주어로 쓰인 동명사(구)는 항상 단수 취급한다.
> **Watching** stars **is** Ben's hobby.

TIP 동명사의 부정은 동명사 앞에 not(never)를 써서 나타낸다.
I'm sorry for **not** **keeping** my promise.   약속을 지키지 못해서 미안하다.

1 동명사 역할 익히기

1 만화책은 재미있다.   →   Comic books   are fun.

만화책을 읽는 것은 재미있다. (read)   →   ______________________   is fun.

2 Jake는 매운 음식을 좋아한다.   → Jake likes   spicy food .

Jake는 매운 음식을 먹는 것을 좋아한다. (eat)   → Jake likes   ______________ .

3 그의 취미는 테니스이다.   → His hobby is   tennis .

그의 취미는 테니스를 치는 것이다. (play)   → His hobby is   ______________ .

2 동명사 형태 적용하기

1 나는 네 친구인 것이 자랑스럽다. (be)

→ I'm proud of __________ your friend.

2 Julie는 K-pop 음악을 듣는 것을 매우 좋아한다. (listen)

→ Julie loves __________ to K-pop music.

3 돈을 낭비하지 않는 것은 좋은 습관이다. (not, waste)

→ __________ __________ money is a good habit.

4 대도시에 사는 것은 때로는 스트레스가 쌓인다. (live)

→ __________ in a big city is sometimes stressful.

5 그가 가장 좋아하는 활동은 그의 개들을 산책시키는 것이다. (walk)

→ His favorite activity is __________ his dogs.

 2 동명사 관용 표현

동명사를 사용한 관용 표현은 다음과 같다.

go -ing	~하러 가다	look forward to -ing	~하기를 고대하다
be busy -ing	~하느라 바쁘다	feel like -ing	~하고 싶다
be used to -ing	~하는 데 익숙하다	How(What) about -ing?	~하는 게 어때?
cannot(can't) help -ing	~하지 않을 수 없다	spend+시간/돈+-ing	~하는 데 시간/돈을 쓰다
have difficulty -ing	~하는 데 어려움을 겪다	be worth -ing	~할 가치가 있다

My dad **is busy preparing** dinner.

I **feel like trying** Indian food today.

I **look forward to going** on a field trip.

That museum **is worth visiting**.

주의 look forward to, be used to 등에 사용된 to는 to부정사를 만드는 to가 아니라 전치사 to로, 뒤에는 동명사가 온다.

She *is used to* **eating** alone. (○)   She *is used to* eat alone. (×)

1 동명사 관용 표현 익히기

1   try   시도해 볼 가치가 있다   → be ___________ ___________

2   visit   방문하기를 고대하다   → look forward ___________ ___________

3   laugh   웃지 않을 수 없다   → cannot ___________ ___________

4   sing   노래 부르고 싶다   → feel ___________ ___________

2 동명사 관용 표현 적용하기

보기	go choose study work

1 Eric은 시험에 대비해 공부하느라 바쁘다.

→ Eric is ___________ ___________ for the exam.

2 산책하러 가는 게 어때?

→ What ___________ ___________ for a walk?

3 나는 친구를 위한 선물을 고르는 데 어려움을 겪었다.

→ I had ___________ ___________ a gift for my friend.

4 James는 늦게까지 일하는 데 익숙하다.

→ James is used ___________ ___________ late.

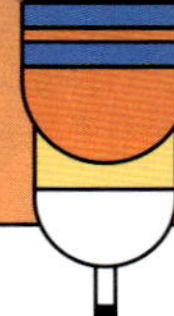

영작 기본 훈련

STEP 1 동명사 문장 **비교하기**

A 동명사 역할 비교하기

1 exercise

ⓐ Dan은 **운동하는 것을** 좋아한다.
Dan likes ________.

ⓑ Dan의 문제는 너무 많이 **운동하는 것**이다.
Dan's problem is ________ too much.

2 speak

ⓐ Kate는 **영어를 말하는 것을** 즐긴다.
Kate enjoys ________ ________.

ⓑ **영어를 말하는 것은** 나에게 쉽지 않다.
________ ________ is not easy for me.

3 help

ⓐ 너는 **우리를 돕는 것을** 꺼리지 않았다.
You didn't mind ________ ________.

ⓑ **우리를 도와준 것에** 대해 너에게 고맙다.
Thank you for ________ ________.

4 play

ⓐ 내 취미는 **축구를 하는 것**이다.
My hobby is ________ ________.

ⓑ **축구를 하는 것은** 나를 행복하게 만든다.
________ ________ makes me happy.

B 동명사 표현 비교하기

1 watch

ⓐ 나는 이 영화를 **보고 싶다.**
I feel ________ ________ this movie.

ⓑ 이 영화를 **보는 게 어때?**
What ________ ________ this movie?

2 surf

ⓐ 이번 주말에 **서핑하러 가자.**
Let's ________ ________ this weekend.

ⓑ 그들은 해변에서 **서핑하느라 바쁘다.**
They are ________ ________ at the beach.

3 eat

ⓐ 그녀는 초밥을 **먹는 것에 익숙하다.**
She is ________ ________ ________ sushi.

ⓑ 나는 초밥을 **먹는 것을 고대하고 있다.**
I'm looking ________ ________ ________ sushi.

4 buy

ⓐ 나는 이 책들을 **사는 데** 100달러를 **썼다.**
I ________ 100 dollars ________ these books.

ⓑ 이 책들은 **살 만한 가치가 있다.**
These books are ________ ________.

STEP **2** 영작 **완성하기**

1 이 앱을 내려받는 게 어때? (download)

→ How ___________ ___________ this app?

2 자전거를 타는 것은 새로운 장소들을 탐방하는 훌륭한 방법이다. (ride, a bike)

→ ___________ ___________ ___________ is a great way to explore new places.

3 우리는 너에게서 소식을 듣기를 고대하고 있다. (hear)

→ We are ___________ ___________ ___________ ___________ from you.

4 나는 친구들과 스키 타러 가는 것을 즐긴다. (enjoy, ski)

→ I ___________ ___________ ___________ with my friends.

5 나는 그들의 결혼식 동안 미소 짓지 않을 수 없었다. (help, smile)

→ I ___________ ___________ ___________ during their wedding.

STEP **3** 배열 **영작하기**

1 나는 새로운 언어를 배우는 것을 잘하지 못한다. not, new languages, at, good, learning

→ I'm ____.

2 사진을 찍는 것은 좋은 취미이다. a, hobby, taking, is, photos, good

→ ____

3 그녀는 옷을 사는 데 많은 돈을 쓴다. buying, spends, she, money, clothes, a lot of

→ ____

4 우리는 그 경기에 질까 봐 두렵다. of, the game, are, we, losing, afraid

→ ____

5 이 소설은 다시 읽을 가치가 있다. worth, this novel, again, reading, is

→ ____

동명사와 to부정사 중 하나만을 목적어로 쓰는 동사가 있다.

동명사를 목적어로 쓰는 동사	enjoy, finish, stop, keep, avoid, give up, mind 등	Jisu *finished* **packing** for the trip. We *kept* **walking** down the street.
to부정사를 목적어로 쓰는 동사	want, hope, plan, decide, learn, expect, agree, need, promise 등	They *plan* **to visit** Tokyo this summer. I *agreed* **to change** the schedule.

주의 stop은 동명사를 목적어로 쓰는 동사로, stop 뒤에 to부정사가 오는 경우에는 목적어가 아니라 '~하기 위해'라는 의미의 부사적
용법으로 사용된 것이다.
She *stopped* **eating** a sandwich.　그녀는 샌드위치 **먹는 것을** 멈췄다.
She *stopped* **to eat** a sandwich.　그녀는 샌드위치를 **먹기 위해** 멈췄다.

1 동명사와 to부정사 목적어 구분하여 쓰기

e.g.	write	쓰는 것을 즐기다	enjoy _____writing_____
1	come	오기로 약속하다	promise _____________
2	drink	마시는 것을 멈추다	stop _____________
3	eat	먹는 것을 피하다	avoid _____________
4	meet	만날 것을 기대하다	expect _____________
5	run	뛰는 것을 포기하다	give up _____________
6	read	계속 읽다	keep _____________

2 동명사와 to부정사 목적어 형태 적용하기

1 우리는 대만으로 여행 가는 것을 계획했다. (travel)　→ We planned _____________ to Taiwan.

2 그들은 시험 준비하는 것을 끝마쳤다. (prepare)　→ They finished _____________ for the test.

3 나는 외국에서 공부하기로 결심했다. (study)　→ I decided _____________ abroad.

4 그는 뒤에 앉는 것을 꺼리지 않는다. (sit)　→ He doesn't mind _____________ in the back.

5 Nancy는 너와 같이 가는 것에 동의했니? (go)　→ Did Nancy agree _____________ with you?

 4 동명사와 to부정사 모두 목적어로 쓰는 동사

A 동명사와 to부정사를 모두 목적어로 쓰는 동사가 있다.

동명사와 to부정사를 모두 목적어로 쓰는 동사	like, love, hate, begin, start, continue 등	I *like* **wearing(to wear)** my blue sweater. Matt *began* **talking(to talk)** about the weather.

B 동명사와 to부정사를 둘 다 목적어로 쓸 수 있지만, 의미가 달라지는 동사가 있다.

forget＋동명사 forget＋to부정사	(과거에) ~한 것을 잊다 (미래에) ~할 것을 잊다	I *forgot* **calling** Brian. I *forgot* **to call** Brian.
remember＋동명사 remember＋to부정사	(과거에) ~한 것을 기억하다 (미래에) ~할 것을 기억하다	I *remembered* **sending** an email to Josh. I *remembered* **to send** an email to Josh.
try＋동명사 try＋to부정사	(시험 삼아) ~해 보다 ~하려고 애쓰다(노력하다)	She *tried* **going** to bed early. She *tried* **to go** to bed early.

1 동명사와 to부정사 목적어 구분하여 쓰기 (둘 다 쓸 수 있는 경우 모두 쓸 것)

e.g.	draw	그리기를 시작하다	start _drawing(to draw)_
1	**visit**	방문한 것을 기억하다	remember ＿＿＿＿＿＿＿
2	**write**	시험 삼아 써 보다	try ＿＿＿＿＿＿＿
3	**walk**	걷는 것을 계속하다	continue ＿＿＿＿＿＿＿
4	**watch**	보는 것을 좋아하다	like ＿＿＿＿＿＿＿
5	**say**	말한 것을 잊다	forget ＿＿＿＿＿＿＿

2 동명사와 to부정사 목적어 형태 적용하기

1 문을 잠그는 것을 잊지 마세요. (lock)　→ Don't forget ＿＿＿＿＿＿＿ the door.

2 그는 설거지하는 것을 싫어한다. (wash)　→ He hates ＿＿＿＿＿＿＿ the dishes.

3 우리는 그 무거운 상자들을 나르려고 애썼다. (carry)　→ We tried ＿＿＿＿＿＿＿ the heavy boxes.

4 눈이 많이 오기 시작했다. (snow)　→ It began ＿＿＿＿＿＿＿ heavily.

영작 기본 훈련

STEP 1 동명사와 to부정사 **비교하기**

A 동사에 따른 목적어 비교하기

1
- ⓐ 그녀는 벽을 칠한다. — She paints the wall.
- ⓑ 그녀는 **벽을 칠하는 것을** 중단했다. — She stopped ___________________.
- ⓒ 그녀는 **벽을 칠하기로** 결심했다. — She decided ___________________.

2
- ⓐ 우리는 우리의 항공편을 예약했다. — We booked our flights.
- ⓑ 우리는 **우리의 항공편을 예약해야** 한다. — We need ___________________.
- ⓒ 우리는 **우리의 항공편을 예약하는 것을** 끝냈다. — We finished ___________________.

3
- ⓐ 그들은 자신들의 음식을 나눈다. — They share their food.
- ⓑ 그들은 **자신들의 음식을 나누는 것을** 즐긴다. — They enjoy ___________________.
- ⓒ 그들은 **자신들의 음식을 나누기로** 동의했다. — They agreed ___________________.

B 동명사와 to부정사 의미 비교하기

1 take
- ⓐ 나는 우산을 **가져간 것을** 잊었다. — I ___________________ my umbrella.
- ⓑ 나는 우산을 **가져갈 것을** 잊었다. — I ___________________ my umbrella.

2 solve
- ⓐ Jane은 그 문제를 **풀려고 노력했다.** — Jane ___________________ the problem.
- ⓑ Jane은 그 문제를 **시험 삼아 풀어 보았다.** — Jane ___________________ the problem.

3 buy
- ⓐ 그는 우유를 좀 **산 것을 기억했다.** — He ___________________ some milk.
- ⓑ 그는 우유를 좀 **살 것을 기억했다.** — He ___________________ some milk.

4 watch
- ⓐ 그들은 일몰을 **보는 것을 멈췄다.** — They ___________________ the sunset.
- ⓑ 그들은 일몰을 **보기 위해 멈췄다.** — They ___________________ the sunset.

STEP **2** 영작 완성하기

1 나는 그것을 비밀로 하기로 약속했다. (promise, keep)

→ I ___________________________ it a secret.

2 그는 사실을 말하는 것을 피했다. (avoid, tell)

→ He ___________________________ the truth.

3 너는 불을 끄는 것을 기억해야 한다. (remember, turn off)

→ You should ___________________________ the lights.

4 그들은 서로에게 눈덩이를 던지는 것을 멈췄다. (stop, throw)

→ They ___________________________ snowballs at each other.

5 Josh는 나에게 이메일 보낼 것을 잊었다. (forget, send)

→ Josh ___________________________ me an email.

STEP **3** 배열 영작하기

1 그녀는 일자리 찾는 것을 포기했다. work, looking for, gave up

→ She ____ .

2 Paul은 그 경기에서 승리하기를 기대한다. the game, to, expects, win

→ Paul ____ .

3 Stella는 비가 올 때 외출하는 것을 싫어했다. to, hated, go out

→ Stella ___________________________ when it rained.

4 볼륨을 낮춰 주시겠어요? you, turning down, mind, the volume, would

→ ____

5 그녀는 너의 졸업식에 참석할 계획이다. attend, plans, your graduation ceremony, to, she

→ ____

집중 훈련 1 틀린 부분 고치기

어법이나 의미가 <u>틀린</u> 부분을 찾아 바르게 고치시오.

집중 훈련 2 영작 완성하기

주어진 말을 활용하여 문장을 완성하시오.

---

01 I'm thinking about join the book club.
나는 독서 동아리에 가입하는 것에 대해 생각 중이다.

_______________ → _______________

02 Sam planned moving into a new apartment.
Sam은 새 아파트로 이사 가는 것을 계획했다.

_______________ → _______________

03 I don't feel like to eat out tonight.
나는 오늘 밤에 외식하고 싶지 않다.

_______________ → _______________

04 He remembered to put his bag on the desk.
그는 자신의 가방을 책상 위에 둔 것을 기억했다.

_______________ → _______________

05 My worst habit is doing not my homework on time.
나의 가장 안 좋은 습관은 숙제를 제때 하지 않는 것이다.

_______________ → _______________

06 My family went to camping last weekend.
나의 가족은 지난 주말에 캠핑하러 갔다.

_______________ → _______________

07 We stopped to walk because it started to rain.
비가 오기 시작해서 우리는 산책하는 것을 멈췄다.

_______________ → _______________

---

08 나는 오늘 점심을 늦게 먹어도 상관없다. (mind, eat)

→ _______________________ lunch late today.

09 그는 그 마라톤에서 달리는 것을 고대하고 있다.
(look forward, run)

→ He is _______________________ in the marathon.

10 이 뉴스 기사는 공유할 가치가 있다. (worth, share)

→ This news article _______________________.

11 그들은 회의에서 그 문제를 논의할 것으로 예상한다.
(expect, discuss)

→ _______________________ the matter in the meeting.

12 나는 휴대 전화로 책을 읽는 데 익숙하다.
(used, read)

→ _______________________ books on my cell phone.

13 나는 그의 문제를 이해하려고 애썼다. (try, understand)

→ _______________________ his problem.

14 우리는 그 슬픈 소식에 울지 않을 수 없었다. (help, cry)

→ _______________________ at the sad news.

집중 훈련 3 통문장 영작하기

주어진 말을 활용하여 영작하시오.

15 Dave는 전화 통화하는 것을 즐기지 않는다.
(enjoy, talk on the phone)

→ _______________________________________

16 우리는 우리의 휴가를 계획하느라 바쁘다.
(busy, plan our vacation)

→ _______________________________________

17 그녀는 엘리베이터 타는 것을 두려워한다.
(be afraid of, take elevators)

→ _______________________________________

18 나는 미스터리를 푸는 것에 흥미가 있다.
(be interested in, solve mysteries)

→ _______________________________________

19 그는 계속해서 혼잣말을 한다. (keep, talk to himself)

→ _______________________________________

20

A 나와 같이 영화 보러 가는 게 어때?
(how, go to the movies, with)

B That sounds great.

→ _______________________________________

21

A Do you know Tom?
B Yes, I do. 나는 그를 파티에서 만난 것을 기억해.
(remember, at the party)

→ _______________________________________

집중 훈련 4 조건 영작하기

우리말과 의미가 같도록 〈조건〉에 맞게 영작하시오.

22 학교 축제에 가는 것은 신난다.

> 조건 1 주어진 말을 활용할 것
> (go to, school festivals, exciting)
> 2 동명사를 반드시 사용할 것
> 3 6단어의 문장으로 서술할 것

→ _______________________________________

23 그는 그의 친구들과 싸우는 것을 피하고 싶었다.

> 조건 1 주어진 말을 활용할 것
> (want, avoid, fight with)
> 2 8단어의 문장으로 쓸 것

→ _______________________________________

24 그녀는 어젯밤에 창문을 닫는 것을 잊었다.

> 조건 1 괄호 안에 주어진 말을 활용할 것
> (forget, close the window)
> 2 동명사 또는 to부정사를 반드시 사용할 것

→ _______________________________________

25 우리는 멕시코 음식을 요리하는 데 두 시간을 썼다.

> 조건 1 주어진 말을 사용할 것
> (spend, hours, Mexican food)
> 2 필요시 형태를 변형할 것
> 3 총 7단어의 문장으로 쓸 것

→ _______________________________________

서술형 1 (3점)

우리말과 의미가 같도록 주어진 말을 활용하여 문장을 완성하시오.

> Helen은 단어를 기억하는 것을 잘한다.
> (remember, words, good)

→ Helen is ＿＿＿＿＿ ＿＿＿＿＿ ＿＿＿＿＿
＿＿＿＿＿.

서술형 2 (2점)

다음 문장에서 어법상 틀린 부분을 찾아 바르게 고쳐 쓰시오.

> Taking care of many dogs are not easy.

＿＿＿＿＿＿＿＿＿ → ＿＿＿＿＿＿＿＿＿

서술형 3 (8점, 각 4점)

우리말과 의미가 같도록 〈조건〉에 맞게 영작하시오.

> (1) 나는 잠드는 데 어려움을 겪는다.

조건 1 주어진 말을 활용하시오.
　　　(difficulty, fall asleep)
　　2 동명사의 관용 표현을 사용하시오.
　　3 5단어의 문장으로 서술하시오.

→ ＿＿＿＿＿＿＿＿＿＿＿＿＿＿＿＿＿

> (2) 그녀는 일찍 일어나는 데 익숙하지 않다.

조건 1 주어진 말을 활용하시오.
　　　(used, get up early)
　　2 동명사의 관용 표현을 사용하시오.
　　3 8단어의 문장으로 서술하시오.

→ ＿＿＿＿＿＿＿＿＿＿＿＿＿＿＿＿＿

서술형 4 (2점)

그림을 보고, 우리말과 의미가 같도록 문장을 완성하시오.

The pizza looked so delicious. I ＿＿＿＿＿ help
＿＿＿＿＿ it. (나는 그것을 먹지 않을 수 없었다.)

서술형 5 NEW (15점)

다음 대화를 읽고, 물음에 답하시오.

Alice	Tony, how about (a) ＿＿＿＿＿ skateboarding?
Tony	Sorry, but I can't. I'm tired. I was busy (b) ＿＿＿＿＿ the piano all day.
Alice	That's too bad.
Tony	I have a competition next Wednesday. I hope (c) ＿＿＿＿＿ it.
Alice	Then you should keep (d) ＿＿＿＿＿ for it.
Tony	You're right. Let's go skateboarding next weekend!
Alice	Sounds good. <u>나는 좋은 소식을 듣기를 고대할게.</u>
Tony	Thank you for (e) ＿＿＿＿＿ so.

(1) 〈보기〉에 주어진 말을 알맞은 형태로 바꿔 (a)~(e)의 빈칸에 쓰시오. (한 번씩만 쓸것) (각 2점)

보기　　say　go　win　practice　prepare

(2) 밑줄 친 우리말을 주어진 말을 사용하여 영작하시오.
　　(8단어로 쓸 것) (5점)

→ ＿＿＿＿＿＿＿＿＿＿＿＿＿＿＿＿＿
(will, look forward, hear, good news)

분사

분사는 동사원형에 -ing 또는 -(e)d를 붙여 형용사처럼 쓰이는 말이다. 분사의 종류에는 현재분사와 과거분사가 있다.

현재분사		과거분사	
「동사원형+-ing」		「동사원형+-(e)d」 또는 불규칙 변화	
~하는, ~하고 있는 〈능동, 진행〉		~된, ~한 〈수동, 완료〉	
boiling water	끓는 물	**boiled** water	끓인 물
a **hiding** dog	숨어 있는 개	**hidden** treasure	숨겨진 보물

Ted wants a **talking** robot for his birthday.   (말하는 로봇)
This bag was made of **recycled** materials.   (재활용된 재료)

1 분사 형태 익히기

1   fall   떨어지는 나뭇잎들   → ___________ leaves
              떨어진 나뭇잎들   → ___________ leaves

2   cook   요리하는 남자   → a ___________ man
              요리된 생선   → a ___________ fish

3   paint   색칠하는 아이   → a ___________ child
               색칠해진 벽   → a ___________ wall

4   grow   자라나는 소년   → a ___________ boy
              성인 남자   → a ___________ man

2 분사 형태 적용하기

1   짖어대는 개 때문에 우리는 잠을 잘 잘 수 없었다. (bark)

→ We couldn't sleep well because of a ___________ dog.

2   그들은 나에게 고장 난 시계를 팔았다. (break)

→ They sold me a ___________ clock.

3   나는 어젯밤 꿈에서 날아다니는 양탄자를 보았다. (fly)

→ I saw a ___________ carpet in my dream last night.

4   그는 멋진 중고차를 샀다. (use)

→ He bought a nice ___________ car.

2 분사의 쓰임

A 분사가 명사를 단독으로 꾸며 줄 때는 명사의 앞에, 다른 단어들과 구를 이루어 수식할 때는 명사의 뒤에 쓴다.

명사 앞에서 수식	Look at the **smiling** girl.	미소 짓는 소녀
명사 뒤에서 수식	Look at the girl **smiling** at Josh.	Josh에게 미소 짓는 소녀

B 분사는 주어나 목적어의 상태 또는 동작을 설명하는 보어 역할을 한다.

주격 보어	You look **depressed** today.	너는 오늘 우울해 보인다.
목적격 보어	I heard someone **calling** my name.	나는 누군가 내 이름을 부르는 것을 들었다.

TIP 분사는 진행형, 완료형, 수동태를 만들 때도 사용된다.

They *are* **playing** basketball. 〈진행형: be동사+현재분사〉
We *have* just **finished** dinner. 〈완료형: have+과거분사〉
The book *was* **written** in French. 〈수동태: be동사+과거분사〉

1 분사 쓰임 익히기

1 이 바구니는 베트남에서 만들어졌다. (make)

→ This basket was ___________ in Vietnam.

2 그 아이들은 바이올린을 연주하고 있다. (play)

→ The children are ___________ the violin.

3 그 피자는 탄 것처럼 보였다. (burn)

→ The pizza looked ___________.

4 너는 웃고 있는 저 소년을 아니? (laugh)

→ Do you know that ___________ boy?

5 우리는 나무 밑에 묻혀 있던 동전 하나를 발견했다. (bury)

→ We found a coin ___________ under the tree.

6 그녀는 여권을 잃어버렸다. (lose)

→ She has ___________ her passport.

7 그 동네에는 문 닫은 상점들이 많이 있었다. (close)

→ There were many ___________ shops in the town.

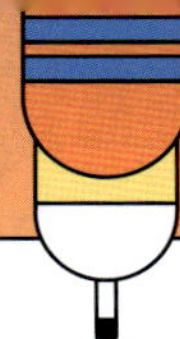

STEP 1 분사 사용하여 문장 확장하기

1 swim

ⓐ 나는 고래들을 보았다.　　　　　I saw whales.

ⓑ 나는 **헤엄치고 있는** 고래들을 보았다.　　　I saw ___________ whales.

2 make

ⓐ 이 수프는 맛있다.　　　　　This soup is delicious.

ⓑ 엄마에 의해 **만들어진** 이 수프는 맛있다.　　　This soup ___________ by my mom is delicious.

3 sit

ⓐ 그 고양이는 조그맣다.　　　　　The cat is tiny.

ⓑ 소파 위에 **앉아 있는** 고양이는 조그맣다.　　　The cat ___________ on the sofa is tiny.

4 lose

ⓐ 그는 자신의 자전거를 찾고 있다.　　　　　He is looking for his bike.

ⓑ 그는 **잃어버린** 자신의 자전거를 찾고 있다.　　　He is looking for his ___________ bike.

5 talk

ⓐ 그 소년은 Tom이다.　　　　　The boy is Tom.

ⓑ 전화 **통화하고 있는** 소년은 Tom이다.　　　The boy ___________ on the phone is Tom.

6 call

ⓐ Sally는 학생이다.　　　　　Sally is a student.

ⓑ Sally는 천재라고 **불리는** 학생이다.　　　Sally is a student ___________ a genius.

7 run

ⓐ 그들은 그 도둑을 잡았다.　　　　　They caught the thief.

ⓑ 그들은 **도망치고 있는** 도둑을 잡았다.　　　They caught the thief ___________ away.

8 grow

ⓐ 그녀는 그 장미들을 좋아한다.　　　　　She likes the roses.

ⓑ 그녀는 자신의 정원에서 **자라고 있는** 장미들을 좋아한다.　　　She likes the roses ___________ in her garden.

STEP ② 영작 완성하기

1 끓는 물을 찻잎 위에 부으세요. (water, boil)

→ Pour the ___________ ___________ over the tea leaves.

2 우리는 200년 전에 지어진 성을 방문했다. (castle, build)

→ We visited a ___________ ___________ two hundred years ago.

3 산꼭대기를 덮고 있는 구름들을 봐. (clouds, cover)

→ Look at the ___________ ___________ the mountain top.

4 그녀는 K-pop 세계에서 떠오르는 스타이다. (star, rise)

→ She is a ___________ ___________ in the K-pop world.

5 너는 그 깨진 꽃병을 치워야 한다. (vase, break)

→ You have to clean up the ___________ ___________.

STEP ③ 배열 영작하기

1 너는 탁자 위에 놓인 돈을 가져가도 된다. on the table, the money, left, take

→ You can ____.

2 그림 한 점이 벽에 걸려 있다. a picture, on the wall, is, hanging

→ There ____.

3 많은 훈련된 동물들이 이 영화에 등장한다. in this movie, trained, appear, animals, many

→ ____

4 그 가수는 소리치고 있는 팬들을 향해 미소 지었다. smiled at, shouting, the singer, the, fans

→ ____

5 그 매장에서 판매된 다이아몬드들은 가짜였다. fake, at the store, the diamonds, were, sold

→ ____

3 감정을 나타내는 분사

A 사람의 감정을 나타내는 동사는 분사 형태로 자주 쓰인다. 이때 '감정을 느끼게 하는'이라는 능동의 의미일 때는 현재분사를, '감정을 느끼게 되는'이라는 수동의 의미일 때는 과거분사를 쓴다.

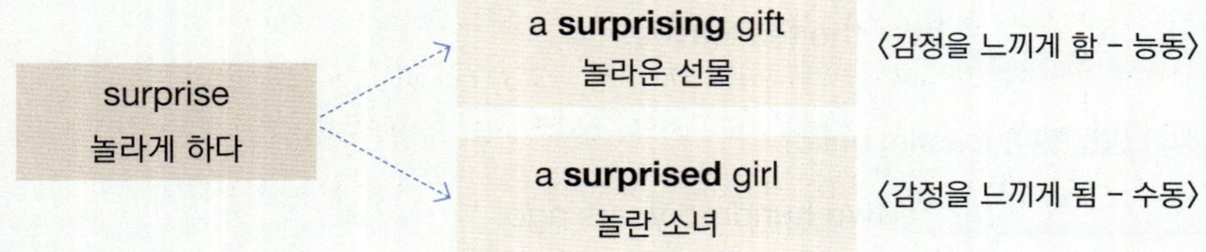

B 감정을 나타내는 분사

동사(~하게 하다)		현재분사(~한 감정을 느끼게 하는)		과거분사(~한 감정을 느끼는)	
surprise	놀라게 하다	surprising	놀라운	surprised	놀란
excite	신나게 만들다	exciting	신나는	excited	신이 난
shock	충격을 주다	shocking	충격적인	shocked	충격 받은
interest	흥미를 끌다	interesting	흥미로운	interested	흥미를 느끼는
satisfy	만족시키다	satisfying	만족스러운	satisfied	만족한
amaze	놀라게 하다	amazing	놀라운	amazed	놀란
bore	지루하게 하다	boring	지루한	bored	지루해하는
disappoint	실망시키다	disappointing	실망스러운	disappointed	실망한

The man's success story was **interesting**.
Kevin was **interested** in the man's success story.

1 감정을 나타내는 분사 형태 익히기

e.g.	shock	충격적인 장면들	_shocking_	scenes
		충격 받은 사람들	_shocked_	people
1	**interest**	흥미를 느낀 아이들	__________	kids
		흥미로운 프로그램들	__________	programs
2	**touch**	감동적인 이야기들	__________	stories
		감동받은 독자들	__________	readers
3	**disappoint**	실망한 팬들	__________	fans
		실망스러운 영화들	__________	movies

2 감정을 나타내는 분사 형태 적용하기

| 보기 | amaze   excite   bore   shock   satisfy

1 어제 축구 경기는 정말 지루했다.

→ The soccer match yesterday was really __________.

2 그 호텔은 만족스러운 식사를 제공했다.

→ The hotel provided a(n) __________ meal.

3 충격 받은 기자는 아무 말도 할 수 없었다.

→ The __________ reporter couldn't say anything.

4 Jane은 가창에 놀라운 재능을 가지고 있다.

→ Jane has a(n) __________ talent for singing.

5 지수는 그 콘서트에 가게 되어 신이 났다.

→ Jisu was __________ to go to the concert.

3 감정을 나타내는 분사 사용하여 문장 완성하기

1 당신은 그 결과에 만족하나요? (satisfy, with)

→ Are you __________ __________ the results?

2 나는 흥미로운 책들을 좀 읽고 싶다. (interest)

→ I'd like to read some __________ __________.

3 우리는 그 식당의 서비스에 실망했다. (disappoint, with)

→ We were __________ __________ the restaurant's service.

4 너는 Tom에 대한 놀라운 소식을 들었니? (surprise, news)

→ Did you hear the __________ __________ about Tom?

5 그는 얼굴에 놀란 표정을 지은 채로 그녀의 말을 들었다. (amaze, look)

→ He listened to her with a(n) __________ __________ on his face.

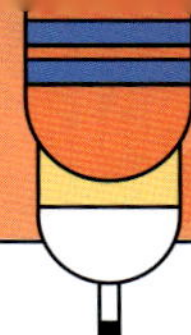

영작 기본 훈련

STEP 1 분사 의미 **비교하기**

1 shock
- ⓐ 우리는 그 사고에 **충격을 받았다.** — We were __________ by the accident.
- ⓑ 그 사고는 **충격적이었다.** — The accident was __________.

2 interest
- ⓐ 그 이야기들은 **흥미로웠다.** — The stories were __________.
- ⓑ 나는 그 이야기들에 **흥미가 있었다.** — I was __________ in the stories.

3 disappoint
- ⓐ 그 팀은 그 경기에 **실망했다.** — The team was __________ with the game.
- ⓑ 그 경기는 **실망스러웠다.** — The game was __________.

4 surprise
- ⓐ 그 불꽃놀이는 **놀라웠다.** — The fireworks were __________.
- ⓑ 그들은 그 불꽃놀이에 **놀랐다.** — They were __________ by the fireworks.

5 excite
- ⓐ 그들의 경기는 **흥미진진하다.** — Their games are __________.
- ⓑ 사람들은 그들의 경기에 **신나 있다.** — People are __________ about their games.

6 bore
- ⓐ Amy는 그의 강연에 **지루해했다.** — Amy was __________ by his lecture.
- ⓑ 그의 강연은 **지루했다.** — His lecture was __________.

7 amaze
- ⓐ 그녀의 친절은 **놀라웠다.** — Her kindness was __________.
- ⓑ 우리는 그녀의 친절에 **놀랐다.** — We were __________ by her kindness.

8 satisfy
- ⓐ 그들은 너의 성과에 **만족했다.** — They were __________ with your performance.
- ⓑ 너의 성과는 **만족스러웠다.** — Your performance was __________.

STEP **2** 배열 영작하기

1 그의 개는 산책하러 가는 것에 항상 신이 나 있다.　go, excited, for a walk, to

→ His dog is always ____ .

2 우리는 매일 밤 똑같은 음식에 싫증 났다.　bored, we, the same food, were, with

→ ____ every night.

3 그 영화의 결말은 만족스럽지 않았다.　wasn't, the mov e, satisfying, of, the ending

→ ____

4 그 프로젝트는 실망스러운 결과로 끝났다.　ended with, the project, results, disappointing

→ ____

5 그 과학자를 직접 만나는 것은 놀라운 일이었다.　the scientist, was, meeting, amazing, in person

→ ____

STEP **3** 부분 영작하기 (분사를 사용할 것)

1 나는 그 구두 가격에 놀랐다. (surprise, by)

→ ________________________________ the price of the shoes.

2 그들은 열대 식물에 관심이 있다. (interest, in)

→ ________________________________ tropical plants.

3 내 여동생은 나에게 충격적인 이야기 하나를 말해 주었다. (shock, story)

→ My sister told me ________________________________ .

4 우리는 학교에서 지루한 과목들을 공부한다. (subjects, bore)

→ We ________________________________ at school.

5 그 등반가들은 에베레스트산에 놀랐다. (Mount Everest, amaze, by)

→ The climbers ________________________________ .

집중 훈련 **1** 틀린 부분 고치기

어법상 틀린 부분을 찾아 바르게 고치시오.

01 They found the box hiding under the bed.

그들은 침대 밑에 숨겨진 상자를 발견했다.

__________ → __________

02 The last scene of the play was surprised.

그 연극의 마지막 장면은 놀라웠다.

__________ → __________

03 She took pictures of fell leaves.

그녀는 떨어진 나뭇잎들의 사진을 찍었다.

__________ → __________

04 I bought some postcards printing in Spain.

나는 스페인에서 인쇄된 엽서 몇 장을 샀다.

__________ → __________

05 He was shocking to see the documentary.

그는 그 다큐멘터리를 보고 충격을 받았다.

__________ → __________

06 The police are looking for the stealing painting.

경찰은 도난당한 그림을 찾고 있다.

__________ → __________

07 She has a dog naming Snoopy.

그녀에게는 Snoopy라고 이름 붙여진 개가 있다.

__________ → __________

집중 훈련 **2** 영작 완성하기

주어진 말을 활용하여 문장을 완성하시오.

08 너는 그 드레스를 입으니 멋져 보인다. (look, amaze)

→ You __________ in that dress.

09 그 상점은 많은 중고 물건들을 판매한다.
(a lot of, use, items)

→ The store sells __________.

10 도와달라고 외치는 남자는 내 이웃이었다.
(shout for help)

→ The man __________ was my neighbor.

11 그녀는 자고 있는 아기를 침대에 눕혔다.
(the, baby, sleep)

→ She put __________ on the bed.

12 우리는 사람들로 가득 찬 연주회장으로 들어갔다.
(fill, with, people)

→ We entered a concert hall __________ __________.

13 그녀의 실패에 대한 소식은 실망스러웠다.
(her failure, disappoint)

→ The news about __________.

14 그 다친 선수는 경기에 출전하지 않았다.
(player, injure)

→ __________ didn't play in the game.

집중 훈련 3 통문장 영작하기
주어진 말을 활용하여 영작하시오.

집중 훈련 4 조건 영작하기
우리말과 의미가 같도록 〈조건〉에 맞게 영작하시오.

15 그 책은 흥미진진한 이야기들로 가득하다.
(be full of, stories, excite)

→ _______________________________________

16 그녀는 성격 검사에 관심이 있다.
(interest, in, personality tests)

→ _______________________________________

17 컴퓨터 게임을 하고 있는 그 소년은 Brian이다.
(play computer games)

→ _______________________________________

18 이것은 영어로 쓰인 소설이다.
(a novel, write, in English)

→ _______________________________________

19 그 학생들은 학교 축제에 만족했다.
(satisfy, with, the school festival)

→ _______________________________________

20

> **A** 너는 그 깨진 창문을 봤니?
> (see, break, window)
> **B** Yes, I did. Who broke it?

→ _______________________________________

21

> **A** How was the 3D movie?
> Was it interesting?
> **B** Not really. 등장인물들이 따분했어.
> (the characters, bore)

→ _______________________________________

22 Vicky와 춤추고 있는 저 소년은 누구니?

> 조건 **1** 주어진 말을 활용할 것
> (who, that boy, dance with)
> **2** 7단어의 문장으로 쓸 것

→ _______________________________________

23 그들은 그 충격적인 소식에 놀랐다.

> 조건 **1** 주어진 말을 활용할 것
> (surprise, by, shock, news)
> **2** 7단어로 쓸 것

→ _______________________________________

24 나는 독일에서 만들어진 손목시계를 샀다.

> 조건 **1** 괄호 안에 주어진 말을 사용할 것
> (a watch, make, in Germany)
> **2** 필요시 형태를 변형할 것
> **3** 7단어의 문장으로 쓸 것

→ _______________________________________

25 그 흥분한 팬들은 경기장으로 달려갔다.

> 조건 **1** 주어진 말을 활용할 것
> (fans, run onto the field)
> **2** exciting과 excited 중 알맞은 말을 쓸 것
> **3** 총 7단어의 문장으로 쓸 것

→ _______________________________________

서술형 1 (6점, 각 3점)

그림을 보고, 주어진 말을 활용하여 문장을 완성하시오.

(1)

→ I like a dish ___________ pad thai. (call)

(2)

→ Look at the boy ___________ on the bench. (sit)

서술형 2 (3점)

다음 문장에서 어법상 틀린 부분을 찾아 바르게 고쳐 쓰시오.

> The results of the experiment were shocked.

___________________ → ___________________

서술형 3 (4점)

우리말과 의미가 같도록 주어진 말을 활용하여 문장을 완성하시오.

> Mark Twain에 의해 쓰인 이 소설은 재미있다.
> (write, interest)

→ This novel ___________ by Mark Twain is ___________.

서술형 4 (4점, 각 2점)

우리말과 의미가 같도록 주어진 말을 알맞은 형태로 쓰시오.

(1) 그는 그림을 그리고 있다. (paint)

→ He is ___________ a picture.

(2) 그는 유명한 화가가 그린 그림 한 점을 샀다. (paint)

→ He bought a picture ___________ by a famous artist.

서술형 5 (5점)

우리말과 의미가 같도록 〈조건〉에 맞게 영작하시오.

> 그 가수의 새로운 노래는 실망스럽다.

조건 1 주어진 말을 활용하시오.
　　　(singer's, disappoint)
　　2 6단어의 문장으로 서술하시오.

→ ___________________________________

서술형 6 NEW (8점, 각 4점)

다음 글의 밑줄 친 우리말과 의미가 같도록 주어진 말을 활용하여 문장을 완성하시오.

> Today is my mom's birthday. My family went to the movies. (1) 그 영화가 흥미진진해서 우리는 그것에 만족했다. (excite, satisfy) After we got back home, we had a party for my mom and gave her presents. (2) 그녀는 그 선물들에 놀랐고 파티에 기뻐했다. (surprise, please)

(1) The movie was ___________, so we were ___________ with it.

(2) She was ___________ at the presents and ___________ with the party.

비교

원급 비교

A 원급 비교는 「as+형용사/부사의 원급+as」의 형태로, 비교하는 두 대상의 정도가 같거나 비슷할 때 쓴다.

as+원급+as	…만큼 ~한/하게	The sunflower is **as tall as** the tree. My laptop is **as good as** Andy's.
not as(so)+원급+as	…만큼 ~하지 않은/않게	Jake's backpack is **not as(so) big as** mine. This sweater is **not as(so) warm as** that one.

B 원급을 이용한 표현

as+원급+as possible = as+원급+as+주어+can	가능한 한 ~한/하게	We need to finish this work **as fast as possible**. = We need to finish this work **as fast as we can**.

TIP 「as+원급+as+주어+can」 구문에서 주어는 문장의 주어를 대명사로 쓴다. 문장의 시제가 현재나 미래인 경우에는 can을, 과거인 경우에는 could를 쓴다.

I *will run* as fast as possible. = I *will run* as fast as **I can**.
John *ran* as fast as possible. = John *ran* as fast as **he could**.

1 원급 비교 형태 익히기

1 thin 종이만큼 얇은 → ＿＿＿＿ ＿＿＿＿ ＿＿＿＿ paper

2 cold 얼음만큼 차가운 → ＿＿＿＿ ＿＿＿＿ ＿＿＿＿ ice

3 quiet 이곳만큼 조용하지 않은 → ＿＿＿＿ ＿＿＿＿ ＿＿＿＿ ＿＿＿＿ here

4 strong Steve만큼 강하지 않은 → ＿＿＿＿ ＿＿＿＿ ＿＿＿＿ ＿＿＿＿ Steve

2 원급 비교 형태 적용하기

보기
high
safe
busy

1 스쿠버 다이빙은 수영만큼 안전하다.

→ Scuba diving is ＿＿＿＿ ＿＿＿＿ ＿＿＿＿ swimming.

2 Lisa는 가능한 한 높이 점프했다.

→ Lisa jumped ＿＿＿＿ ＿＿＿＿ ＿＿＿＿ ＿＿＿＿.

3 나는 지난주만큼 바쁘지는 않다.

→ I'm ＿＿＿＿ ＿＿＿＿ ＿＿＿＿ ＿＿＿＿ last week.

 배수 비교

'…보다 (몇) 배 더 ~한/하게'라는 의미를 나타낼 때는 배수를 나타내는 표현인 배수사를 「as+원급+as」 앞에 쓰며,
「배수사+비교급+than」으로 바꿔 쓸 수 있다.

배수사+as+원급+as = 배수사+비교급+than	…보다 (몇) 배 더 ~한/하게	The tree was **three times as tall as** the kid. = The tree was **three times taller than** the kid.

TIP 배수를 나타내는 표현에서 '두 배'는 twice로 나타내고, 세 배'부터는 「기수+times」로 쓴다.
twice는 「twice+as+원급+as」의 형태로만 쓰는 것어 유의한다.

twice(두 배), three times(세 배), four times(네 배)

---

1 배수 비교 **형태 익히기** (원급을 이용할 것)

e.g.	long	그 연필만큼 긴	__as__	__long__	__as__	the pencil
		그 연필보다 두 배 더 긴	__twice__ __as__	__long__	__as__	the pencil
1	fast	너만큼 빨리				you
		너보다 세 배 더 빨리				you
2	large	내 방만큼 큰				my room
		내 방보다 두 배 더 큰				my room
3	expensive	그 셔츠만큼 비싼				the shirt
		그 셔츠보다 네 배 더 비싼				the shirt

---

2 배수 비교 **형태 적용하기** (원급을 이용할 것)

1 이 책은 저 책보다 다섯 배 더 두껍다. (thick)

→ This book is ___________ ___________ ___________ ___________ ___________ that one.

2 그는 Tom보다 세 배 더 빨리 그 문제를 풀었다. (quickly)

→ He solved the problem ___________ ___________ ___________ ___________ Tom.

3 너의 가방이 내 것보다 두 배 더 무겁다. (heavy)

→ Your bag is ___________ ___________ ___________ mine.

4 나의 아버지는 나보다 세 배 더 나이가 많다. (old)

→ My father is ___________ ___________ ___________ ___________ me.

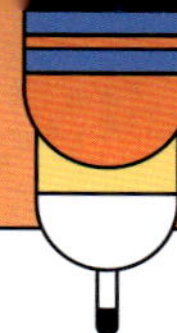

영작 기본 훈련

STEP 1 원급 비교 의미 **확장하기**

1
ⓐ Sally는 어리다.
Sally is young.

ⓑ Sally는 내 남동생**만큼 어리다.**
Sally is __________ __________ __________ my brother.

2
ⓐ 그는 키가 작지 않다.
He is not short.

ⓑ 그는 나**만큼 키가 작지 않다.**
He is __________ __________ __________ __________ me.

3
ⓐ 빨리 돌아와라.
Come back soon.

ⓑ **가능한 한 빨리** 돌아와라.
Come back __________ __________ __________ __________.

4
ⓐ 우리 개는 크다.
Our dog is big.

ⓑ 우리 개는 지나의 개**보다 세 배 더 크다.**
Our dog is __________ __________ __________ __________ __________ Jina's.

5
ⓐ 그 치타는 빨리 달렸다.
The cheetah ran fast.

ⓑ 그 치타는 자동차**만큼 빨리** 달렸다.
The cheetah ran __________ __________ __________ a car.

6
ⓐ 내 수학 점수는 높다.
My math score is high.

ⓑ 내 수학 점수는 내 영어 점수**보다 두 배 더 높다.**
My math score is __________ __________ __________ __________ my English score.

7
ⓐ 그녀는 천천히 말했다.
She talked slowly.

ⓑ 그녀는 **가능한 한 천천히** 말했다.
She talked __________ __________ __________ __________ __________.

8
ⓐ 나의 이모는 건강하지 않다.
My aunt is not healthy.

ⓑ 나의 이모는 나의 엄마**만큼 건강하지 않다.**
My aunt is __________ __________ __________ __________ my mom.

STEP 2 문장 전환하기

1 Susan sings like a professional singer.

→ Susan sings ________ ________ ________ a professional singer. (well)

2 These slippers are 100 dollars. Those sneakers are 100 dollars, too.

→ These slippers are ________ ________ ________ those sneakers. (expensive)

3 We should work out as regularly as possible.

→ We should work out ________ ________ ________ ________ ________. (can)

4 This white skirt is 45 centimeters long. That black one is 90 centimeters long.

→ That black skirt is ________ ________ ________ ________ this white one. (twice, long)

5 The midterm was difficult, but the final exam was more difficult.

→ The midterm was ________ ________ ________ ________ the final exam. (not, difficult)

STEP 3 배열 영작하기

1 내 여동생은 나만큼 수줍어하지 않는다. shy, not, me, so, as, is

→ My sister ____.

2 실제 비행기는 이 모형 비행기보다 삼십 배 더 크다. this model one, is, big, times, as, as, thirty

→ The real airplane ____.

3 이 수영장은 어린이용 수영장보다 네 배 더 깊다. is, times, the kids' pool, as, as, deep, four

→ This pool ____.

4 그 아이는 자신이 할 수 있는 한 멀리 공을 찼다. as, kicked, as, far, could, the ball, he

→ The child ____.

5 Brian은 가능한 한 일찍 일어난다. as, gets up, Brian, possible, early, as

→ ____.

3 비교급 비교

A 비교급은 정도의 차이가 있는 두 대상을 비교하여 '…보다 더 ~한/하게'라는 의미를 나타낼 때 쓴다.

비교급+than	…보다 더 ~한/하게

I am **taller than** you.
This jacket is **more expensive than** that coat.

> **TIP** 비교급 앞에 much, even, still, far, a lot 등을 써서 '훨씬'이라는 의미로 비교급을 강조할 수 있다. very는 형용사나 부사의 원래 형태인 원급을 강조할 때 사용하고, 비교급을 강조할 때는 쓰지 않는다.
>
> Bob is *very* fast.   Bob is *much* **faster** than me.

B 비교급을 이용한 표현

the+비교급 ~, the+비교급 …	~할수록 더 …하다
비교급+and+비교급	점점 더 ~한/하게

The older she grew, **the wiser** she became.

The hole is getting **larger and larger**.
The song became **more and more popular**.

비교급의 형태가 「more + 원급」인 경우에는 「more and more + 원급」으로 쓴다.

1 비교급 비교 형태 익히기

1 cool | 어제보다 더 시원한 | → ___________ ___________ yesterday

2 famous | 그보다 더 유명한 | → ___________ ___________ ___________ him

3 good | 이 품목보다 더 좋은 | → ___________ ___________ this item

4 quietly | 그녀보다 더 조용히 말하다 | → speak ___________ ___________ ___________ her

2 비교급 비교 형태 적용하기

1 이 운동화가 저 운동화보다 더 편하다. (comfortable)

→ These sneakers are ___________ ___________ ___________ those ones.

2 세상이 점점 더 작아지고 있다. (small)

→ The world is getting ___________ ___________ ___________.

3 네가 더 많이 웃을수록 너는 더 행복하게 느낄 것이다. (much, happy)

→ ___________ ___________ you laugh, ___________ ___________ you will feel.

4 최상급 비교

A 최상급은 세 가지 이상을 비교하여 그중 하나가 '가장 ~한/하게'라는 의미를 나타낼 때 쓴다.

the+최상급	가장 ~한/하게	Judy is **the fastest** *of* all runners. Safety is **the most important** thing *in* this class.

TIP 최상급 문장에서 of 뒤에는 주로 비교 대상이, in 뒤에는 장소나 범위가 온다.

This is **the most expensive** smartphone *of* the three. 〈of＋비교 대상: 복수명사, 숫자, 기간 등〉
This is **the most expensive** smartphone *in* the shop. 〈in＋장소/범위의 단수명사〉

B 최상급을 이용한 표현

one of the+최상급+복수명사	가장 ~한 … 중 하나	He is **one of the most famous singers** in the world.

1 최상급 비교 형태 익히기

1 **funny** 가장 웃기는 영화 → __________ __________ movie

2 **diligent** 가장 부지런한 소년 → __________ __________ __________ boy

3 **bad** 가장 안 좋은 습관 → __________ __________ habit

4 **dangerous** 가장 위험한 운동 → __________ __________ __________ sport

5 **nice** 가장 착한 사람 → __________ __________ person

6 **smart** 가장 똑똑한 소녀 → __________ __________ girl

2 최상급 비교 형태 적용하기

1 이것은 이 가게에서 가장 비싼 컴퓨터이다. (expensive)

→ This is __________ __________ __________ computer in this store.

2 목성은 태양계에서 가장 큰 행성이다. (large)

→ Jupiter is __________ __________ planet in the solar system.

3 Mark는 그의 팀에서 가장 힘센 선수들 중 한 명이다. (strong)

→ Mark is one of __________ __________ players on his team.

4 파스타는 그 식당에서 가장 맛있는 요리들 중 하나이다. (delicious)

→ Pasta is one of __________ __________ __________ dishes at the restaurant.

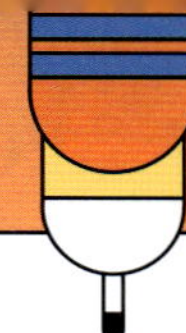

영작 기본 훈련

STEP 1 비교급·최상급 비교 의미 비교하기

1

ⓐ 2월은 짧다.
February is short.

ⓑ 2월은 다른 달들**보다 더 짧다**.
February is ＿＿＿＿ ＿＿＿＿ the other months.

ⓒ 2월은 **가장 짧은** 달이다.
February is ＿＿＿＿ ＿＿＿＿ month.

2

ⓐ 나는 바쁘다.
I'm busy.

ⓑ 나는 너**보다 더 바쁘다**.
I'm ＿＿＿＿ ＿＿＿＿ you.

ⓒ 나는 요즘 **점점 더 바빠지고** 있다.
I'm getting ＿＿＿＿ ＿＿＿＿ ＿＿＿＿ these days.

3

ⓐ 이 소설은 재미있다.
This novel is interesting.

ⓑ 이 소설은 그 영화**보다 더 재미있다**.
This novel is ＿＿＿＿ ＿＿＿＿ ＿＿＿＿ the movie.

ⓒ 이 소설이 그 세 권 중에 **가장 재미있다**.
This novel is ＿＿＿＿ ＿＿＿＿ ＿＿＿＿ of the three.

4

ⓐ 오늘은 덥다.
Today is hot.

ⓑ 오늘은 어제**보다 더 덥다**.
Today is ＿＿＿＿ ＿＿＿＿ yesterday.

ⓒ 오늘은 일 년 중 **가장 더운 날들** 중 하루이다.
Today is ＿＿＿＿ ＿＿＿＿ ＿＿＿＿ ＿＿＿＿ days
of the year.

5

ⓐ 깨끗한 공기는 중요하다.
Clean air is important.

ⓑ 깨끗한 공기는 **점점 더 중요해지고** 있다.
Clean air is getting ＿＿＿＿ ＿＿＿＿ ＿＿＿＿ ＿＿＿＿.

ⓒ 깨끗한 공기는 **가장 중요한 것들** 중 하나이다.
Clean air is ＿＿＿＿ ＿＿＿＿ ＿＿＿＿ ＿＿＿＿
＿＿＿＿ things.

6

ⓐ 그는 열심히 공부했다.
He studied hard.

ⓑ 그는 나보다 **훨씬 더 열심히** 공부했다.
He studied ＿＿＿＿ ＿＿＿＿ ＿＿＿＿ me.

ⓒ 그가 **더 열심히** 공부할수록, 그의 성적은 **더 좋아졌다**.
＿＿＿＿ ＿＿＿＿ he studied, ＿＿＿＿ ＿＿＿＿ his
grades became.

STEP **2** 배열 영작하기

1 부산은 한국에서 가장 큰 도시들 중 한 곳이다. [cities, biggest, one, in Korea, the, is, of]

→ Busan ____ .

2 네가 더 많이 연습할수록 너는 더 잘할 것이다. [better, you, the, do, will]

→ The more you practice, ________________________________ .

3 그녀는 언니보다 더 천천히 운전한다. [drives, slowly, she, her sister, more, than]

→ ____

4 그 가게는 점점 더 붐비게 될 것이다. [more, the store, crowded, and, will, more, get]

→ ____

5 그의 생각은 이것보다 훨씬 더 창의적이다. [far, than, s, more, his idea, creative, this one]

→ ____

STEP **3** 부분 영작하기

1 그 아기는 점점 더 크게 울었다. (loud, cry)

→ The baby ________________________________ .

2 그의 새 차는 그의 예전 차보다 더 비싸다. (expensive, his old one)

→ His new car ________________________________ .

3 그 울타리는 그 아이보다 훨씬 더 높다. (tall, the kid)

→ The fence ________________________________ .

4 그것은 이 오락실에서 가장 신나는 게임들 중 하나이다. (exciting, game)

→ ________________________________ in this arcade.

5 네가 더 많이 운동할수록 너는 더 건강해진다. (exercise, much, healthy)

→ ________________________________ you become.

집중 훈련 1 틀린 부분 고치기
어법상 **틀린** 부분을 찾아 바르게 고치시오.

집중 훈련 2 영작 완성하기
주어진 말을 활용하여 문장을 완성하시오.

01 Today was busiest day of the year.
오늘은 일 년 중 가장 바쁜 날이었다.

___________ → ___________

02 She cooks as better as her mother.
그녀는 그녀의 어머니만큼 요리를 잘한다.

___________ → ___________

03 Happiness is most important than money.
행복은 돈보다 더 중요하다.

___________ → ___________

04 Today is so not cold as yesterday.
오늘은 어제만큼 춥지는 않다.

___________ → ___________

05 She solved one of the most difficult math problem in the world.
그녀는 세계에서 가장 어려운 수학 문제들 중 하나를 풀었다.

___________ → ___________

06 These shoes are twice big as my father's.
이 신발은 내 아버지의 신발보다 두 배 더 크다.

___________ → ___________

07 This pencil is very sharper than that one.
이 연필은 저것보다 훨씬 더 뾰족하다.

___________ → ___________

08 Tina는 오늘 아침에 Jim보다 더 늦게 학교에 왔다. (late)

→ Tina came to school ___________ this morning.

09 이 스카프는 깃털만큼 가볍다. (light, a feather)

→ This scarf is ___________.

10 그 TV 시리즈는 점점 더 흥미로워지고 있다. (interesting)

→ The TV series is getting ___________ ___________.

11 그 불꽃놀이는 영화만큼 멋졌다. (cool, a movie)

→ The fireworks display was ___________ ___________.

12 겨울 축제는 그 나라에서 가장 인기 있는 축제이다. (popular, festival)

→ The Winter Carnival is ___________ ___________ in the country.

13 그는 더 오래 잘수록 더 피곤하게 느꼈다. (long, tired)

→ ___________ he slept, ___________ he felt.

14 그는 세계에서 가장 유명한 배우들 중 한 명이다. (one, famous, actor)

→ He is ___________ in the world.

집중 훈련 **3** 통문장 영작하기
주어진 말을 활용하여 영작하시오.

15 가능한 한 자주 손을 씻어라. (often, possible)

→ ______________________________

16 그녀의 방은 내 방보다 세 배 더 크다.
(room, large, mine, than)

→ ______________________________

17 Leon은 그의 팀에서 최고의 선수이다.
(good, player, on his team)

→ ______________________________

18 그의 점수는 내 점수보다 두 배 더 높다.
(his score, high, as, mine)

→ ______________________________

19 네가 더 일찍 시작할수록 너는 더 일찍 끝낼 것이다.
(early, start, will finish)

→ ______________________________

20
A This beach is so amazing.
B Right. 그것은 세계에서 가장 아름다운 해변들 중 하나야. (beautiful, beach, in the world)

→ ______________________________

21
A Is the Moon as big as the Earth?
B No. 지구는 달보다 훨씬 더 커.
(the Earth, big)

→ ______________________________

집중 훈련 **4** 조건 영작하기
우리말과 의미가 같도록 〈조건〉에 맞게 영작하시오.

22 날씨가 점점 더 따뜻해지고 있다.

조건 **1** 주어진 말을 활용할 것
(the weather, get, warm)
2 현재진행형을 사용할 것
3 7단어의 문장으로 쓸 것

→ ______________________________

23 이것은 이 도시에서 가장 높은 건물이다.

조건 **1** 주어진 말을 활용할 것
(tall, building, in this city)
2 8단어의 문장으로 쓸 것

→ ______________________________

24 이 꽃병은 저 접시보다 네 배 더 비싸다.

조건 **1** 괄호 안에 주어진 말을 사용할 것
(this vase, expensive, that dish)
2 as를 포함할 것
3 10단어로 쓸 것

→ ______________________________

25 나는 가능한 한 분명하게 말하려고 노력했다.

조건 **1** 「as+원급+as」 구문을 사용할 것
2 〈보기〉에 주어진 말을 활용할 것
3 총 9단어의 과거시제 문장으로 쓸 것

보기 | try to speak | clearly | can

→ ______________________________

서술형 1 　(2점)

우리말과 의미가 같도록 주어진 말을 활용하여 문장을 완성하시오.

> 겨울이 오면서 낮이 점점 더 짧아진다.

→ As winter comes, the days get __________ __________ __________. (short)

서술형 2 　(4점)

우리말과 의미가 같도록 〈조건〉에 맞게 영작하시오.

> 그는 나의 학교에서 가장 재능 있는 학생들 중 한 명이다.

조건　1　주어진 말을 사용하시오.
　　　　　(talented, in my school)
　　　　2　11단어의 문장으로 서술하시오.

→ ________________________________

서술형 3 NEW 　(6점, 각 2점)

다음 표를 보고, 〈조건〉에 맞게 문장을 완성하시오.

Room Type	Room Size (square meters)	Room Rate (per night)
Standard	12	$ 70
Superior	20	$ 65 (special sale)
Deluxe	25	$ 120

조건　1　최상급을 사용하시오.
　　　　2　주어진 단어 중 필요한 것을 골라 활용하시오.
　　　　　(cheap, small, large)

(1) The standard room is __________ room.

(2) The superior room is __________ room.

(3) The deluxe room is __________ room.

서술형 4 　(6점, 각 3점)

그림을 보고, 주어진 말을 사용하여 문장을 완성하시오.

(1)

→ My hair is __________________________. (long, as, hers)

(2)

→ We ran __________________________ to catch the bus. (fast, possible)

서술형 5 　(12점, 각 4점)

다음 글의 밑줄 친 우리말을 영작하시오. (tall을 사용할 것)

> 　There are a lot of trees and flowers in my grandma's garden. One tree in the garden stands out from the rest. (1)그것은 정원에서 가장 키가 큰 나무이다. My grandma planted the tree when I was a little girl. (2)그때 그것은 나만큼 키가 크지 않았다. (3)지금 그것은 나보다 더 훨씬 더 키가 크다. On sunny days, we like to sit under the tree.

(1) It is __________________________.

(2) __________________________ then.

(3) Now, __________________________.

접속사

등위접속사는 문법적으로 대등한 단어와 단어, 구와 구, 절과 절을 연결하는 접속사이다.

and, but, or, so	Susan **and** Frank are my old friends. 단어 단어 We can go there by bus **or** by subway. 구 구 I was tired, **but** I finished reading the book. 절 절 It was cold outside, **so** they stayed home. 절 절

and, but, or와 달리 so는 절과 절만 연결한다.

1 알맞은 등위접속사 쓰기

1 그는 나에게 그의 공책을 빌려주었지만, 나는 그것을 잃어버렸다.

→ He lent me his notebook, ＿＿＿＿＿ I lost it.

2 Jane은 Matt과 그의 친구들을 파티에 초대했다.

→ Jane invited Matt ＿＿＿＿＿ his friends to the party.

3 나는 오늘 밤이나 내일 아침에 너를 만날 수 있다.

→ I can meet you tonight ＿＿＿＿＿ tomorrow morning.

4 날이 어두워지고 있어서 우리는 불을 켰다.

→ It was getting dark, ＿＿＿＿＿ we turned on the lights.

2 등위접속사 형태 적용하기

1 그 가죽 가방은 멋지지만 비싸다. (nice, expensive)

→ The leather bag is ＿＿＿＿＿ ＿＿＿＿＿ ＿＿＿＿＿.

2 너는 그것을 산 거니, 아니면 만든 거니? (make)

→ Did you buy it ＿＿＿＿＿ ＿＿＿＿＿ ＿＿＿＿＿?

3 그들은 저녁에 TV를 보았고 아이스크림을 먹었다. (eat ice cream)

→ They watched TV ＿＿＿＿＿ ＿＿＿＿＿ ＿＿＿＿＿ ＿＿＿＿＿ in the evening.

4 그녀는 매우 사려 깊어서 모두가 그녀를 사랑한다. (everyone, love)

→ She is very considerate, ＿＿＿＿＿ ＿＿＿＿＿ ＿＿＿＿＿ ＿＿＿＿＿.

2 상관접속사

상관접속사는 두 개 이상의 단어가 짝을 이루어 쓰이는 접속사이다.

both A and B	A와 B 둘 다	**Both** my bag **and** my cap are wet.
not A but B	A가 아니라 B	I'm **not** tired **but** hungry.
not only A but (also) B = B as well as A	A뿐만 아니라 B도	**Not only** Karen **but also** Tony was late for the class. = Tony **as well as** Karen was late for the class.
either A or B	A나 B 둘 중 하나	He will **either** walk **or** take the bus to school.
neither A nor B	A도 B도 아닌	**Neither** Ben **nor** Joan passed the test.

주의 상관접속사가 주어로 쓰일 경우 「both A and B」는 복수 취급하고, 나머지는 B에 수 일치시킨다.
Both you **and** Amy **have** to go there.   **Either** you **or** Amy **has** to go there.

1 상관접속사 의미 익히기

e.g. **both** bread **and** milk   →   빵과 우유 둘 다

1 children **as well as** adults   →   ______________________

2 **not** English **but** French   →   ______________________

3 **not only** delicious **but also** healthy   →   ______________________

4 **neither** mine **nor** yours   →   ______________________

2 상관접속사 형태 적용하기

1 나는 영화를 보거나 음악을 듣고 싶다.

→ I want to __________ watch a movie __________ listen to music.

2 Alex는 내게 전화하지도 문자를 보내지도 않는다.

→ Alex __________ calls me __________ texts me.

3 공부하는 것과 친구를 사귀는 것 둘 다 많은 노력이 필요하다.

→ __________ studying __________ making friends require a lot of efforts.

4 나의 할아버지는 작가가 아니라 교수이다.

→ My grandfather is __________ a writer __________ a professor.

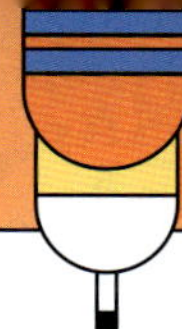

영작 기본 훈련

1 He had no money. He couldn't take the bus.

→ He had no money, __________ __________ __________ __________ the bus.

2 The soup is delicious. The soup is too salty.

→ The soup is __________ __________ __________ __________.

3 We may cook dinner. Or we may order pizza.

→ We may cook dinner __________ __________ __________.

4 I have to study math. I have to study science, too.

→ I have to study __________ __________ __________ __________.

5 She is not angry. She is disappointed.

→ She is __________ __________ __________ __________.

6 We've never been to Spain. We've never been to France, either.

→ We've been to __________ __________ __________ __________.

7 Amy is smart. She is also kind.

→ Amy is __________ __________ __________ __________.

8 You can take the subway. Or you can take a taxi.

→ You can take __________ __________ __________ __________.

STEP 2 배열 영작하기

1 나는 그녀를 기다렸지만, 그녀는 나타나지 않았다. she, waited for, I, show up, didn't, her, but

→ ____

2 내 남동생은 축구와 농구 둘 다 좋아한다. soccer, and, likes, basketball, both, my brother

→ ____

3 너나 Tony 둘 중 한 사람이 그 보고서를 끝내야 한다. Tony, you, or, finish the report, either, has to

→ ____

4 비가 올 뿐만 아니라 춥다. is, well, cold, it, as, rainy, as

→ ____

5 이 카메라는 무겁지도 비싸지도 않다. expensive, nor, this camera, neither, is, heavy

→ ____

STEP 3 부분 영작하기

1 하이킹은 몸과 마음 둘 다에 좋다. (good for, body, mind)

→ Hiking ______________________________________.

2 이 이야기는 허구가 아니라 사실이다. (fiction, fact, but)

→ This story ___________________________________.

3 우리는 오늘 오후에 외식하거나 쇼핑하러 갈 수 있다. (eat out, go shopping)

→ _________________________________ this afternoon.

4 나는 비밀번호를 잊어버려서 이메일을 확인할 수 없다. (check my email)

→ I forgot my password, ________________________.

5 그는 꽃뿐만 아니라 케이크도 샀다. (some flowers, a cake, also)

→ He ____.

that은 문장 안에서 주어, 목적어, 보어 역할을 하는 명사절을 이끄는 접속사로 '~라는 것'으로 해석한다.

주어	**That** they will get married is surprising. → **It** is surprising **that** they will get married. 　가주어　　　　　　　　　　　　진주어
목적어	He said **that** he could come.
보어	The fact is **that** he was not there.

--------→ that절이 주어로 쓰일 때는 주어 자리에 가주어 it을 쓰고 that절은 뒤로 보낸다.

TIP that절이 목적어로 쓰인 경우 접속사 that은 생략할 수 있다.
Everyone knows (**that**) he likes you.

---

1 접속사 that 사용하여 **문장 쓰기**

e.g.
She can't come to the party.
→ The problem is ________ that she can't come to the party ________.

1 He won the race.

→ It was lucky ________________________________.

2 The room was empty.

→ They said ________________________________.

3 We have enough time.

→ The good thing is ________________________.

---

2 접속사 that 사용하여 **문장 완성하기**

1 그녀가 그 시험에 통과했다는 것이 놀라웠다. (pass)

→ It was amazing __________ __________ __________ the test.

2 그는 내가 그에게 전화했다는 것을 알고 있다. (know, call)

→ He __________ __________ __________ __________ him.

3 그의 장점은 그가 솔직하다는 것이다. (strength)

→ __________ __________ __________ __________ he is honest.

 4 부사절을 이끄는 접속사

시간, 이유, 조건 등을 나타내는 접속사는 문장 안에서 부사 역할을 하는 부사절을 이끈다.

시간	before (~하기 전에)	I'll come back **before** it gets dark.
	after (~한 후에)	Let's go on a trip **after** the exams end.
	when (~할 때)	**When** I woke up, I felt hungry.
	while (~하는 동안)	**While** you're eating, don't speak.
이유	because (~하기 때문에)	I was late **because** I missed the train.
	as (~하기 때문에)	**As** I was sick, I stayed in bed.
조건	if (만약 ~하면)	I won't go camping **if** it rains.
	unless (만약 ~하지 않으면)	**Unless** we hurry, we won't be on time. (→ **If** we do **not** hurry, we won't be on time.)

TIP 시간이나 조건을 나타내는 부사절에서는 현재시제를 써서 미래의 일을 나타낸다.

I'll leave **when** Daniel **arrives**. (○)
I'll leave **when** Daniel will arrive. (×)

1 알맞은 부사절 접속사 쓰기

1 그가 그녀를 만났을 때 → ___________ he met her

2 네가 원하면 → ___________ you want

3 눈이 내렸기 때문에 → ___________ it snowed

4 내가 졸업한 후에 → ___________ I graduate

2 부사절 접속사 사용하여 문장 완성하기

1 그가 피아노를 치고 있는 동안 나는 숙제를 했다. (play)

→ I did my homework ___________ ___________ ___________ ___________ the piano.

2 너는 지하철을 타지 않으면 늦을 것이다. (take)

→ You will be late ___________ ___________ ___________ the subway.

3 우리는 그 나라를 방문하기 전에 그 나라의 문화에 대해 배웠다. (visit)

→ ___________ ___________ ___________ the country, we learned about its culture.

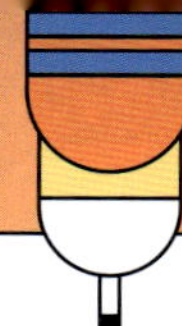

영작 기본 훈련

STEP 1 접속사 사용하여 의미 확장하기

A 명사절 접속사로 의미 확장하기

1
- **ⓐ** 나는 그녀를 안다.
  I know her.　(a fashion model)
- **ⓑ** 나는 **그녀가 패션모델이라는 것**을 안다.
  I know ________________________.

2
- **ⓐ** 문제는 그의 목소리이다.
  The problem is his voice.　(too loud)
- **ⓑ** 문제는 **그의 목소리가 너무 크다는 것**이다.
  The problem is ________________________.

3
- **ⓐ** 그의 죽음은 충격적이었다.
  His death was shocking.　(die)
- **ⓑ** **그가 사망했다는 것**은 충격적이었다.
  It was shocking ________________________.

B 부사절 접속사로 의미 확장하기

1
- **ⓐ** 나는 이를 닦는다.
  I brush my teeth.　(go to bed)
- **ⓑ** **나는 잠자리에 들기 전에** 이를 닦는다.
  I brush my teeth ________________________.

2
- **ⓐ** 외출하자.
  Let's go out.　(bored)
- **ⓑ** **만일 네가 지루하면** 외출하자.
  Let's go out ________________________.

3
- **ⓐ** 어두웠다.
  It was dark.　(get home)
- **ⓑ** **내가 집에 도착했을 때** 어두웠다.
  It was dark ________________________.

4
- **ⓐ** 그녀는 울었다.
  She cried.　(fail the test)
- **ⓑ** **그녀는 시험에 떨어져서** 울었다.
  She cried ________________________.

5
- **ⓐ** 그는 음악을 들었다.
  He listened to music.　(exercise)
- **ⓑ** **그는 운동을 하고 있는 동안** 음악을 들었다.
  He listened to music ________________________.

STEP ② 영작 완성하기

1 네가 외출할 때 전등을 꺼라. (go out)

→ Turn off the light __________ __________ __________ __________.

2 만약 네가 아침 식사를 하지 않으면 배고플 것이다. (eat breakfast)

→ __________ __________ __________ __________, you will be hungry.

3 내가 자고 있는 동안 내 여동생은 TV를 봤다. (sleep)

→ My sister watched TV __________ __________ __________ __________.

4 나는 모두가 평화롭게 살기를 바란다. (everyone, in peace)

→ I hope __________ __________ __________ __________ __________.

5 날이 추워서 우리는 건물로 들어갔다. (it, cold)

→ __________ __________ __________ __________, we entered the building.

STEP ③ 배열 영작하기

1 네가 이 책을 읽고 싶으면 내가 너에게 그것을 빌려줄게. read, want, you, to, if, this book

→ ________________________________, I will lend it to you.

2 내 형이 취직을 했다는 것이 놀랍다. my brother, that, it, amazing, got, is, a job

→ ________________________________

3 너는 수영하기 전에 준비 운동을 해야 한다. warm up, you, swim, you, before, have to

→ ________________________________

4 만약 네가 친구가 없다면 외로울 것이다. have, feel, you, no friends, you, lonely, will, if

→ ________________________________

5 슬픈 것은 내가 그를 이해할 수 없다는 것이다. the sad thing, can't, is, I, understand, that, him

→ ________________________________

집중 훈련 1 틀린 부분 고치기
어법이나 의미가 <u>틀린</u> 부분을 찾아 바르게 고치시오.

집중 훈련 2 영작 완성하기
주어진 말을 활용하여 문장을 완성하시오.

01
I couldn't borrow the book so the library was closed.
도서관이 문을 닫아서 나는 그 책을 빌릴 수 없었다.

_______________ → _______________

02
Neither Frank or Ted will come to the party.
Frank도 Ted도 그 파티에 오지 않을 것이다.

_______________ → _______________

03
He ate cake before he had dinner.
그는 저녁을 먹은 후에 케이크를 먹었다.

_______________ → _______________

04
I'll call you when I will get home.
내가 집에 도착할 때 너에게 전화할게.

_______________ → _______________

05
Both my brother and my sister wants a cat.
내 남동생과 여동생 둘 다 고양이를 원한다.

_______________ → _______________

06
He enjoys watching movies and read books on weekends.
그는 주말에 영화 보는 것과 책 읽는 것을 즐긴다.

_______________ → _______________

07
We may be late unless we don't walk faster.
우리가 더 빨리 걷지 않으면 늦을지도 모른다.

_______________ → _______________

08 그가 나를 방문했을 때 나는 저녁을 먹고 있었다. (visit)

→ I was having dinner _______________.

09 나는 공포 영화를 좋아하지만, 그는 그것들을 좋아하지 않는다. (like)

→ I like horror movies, _______________
_______________.

10 그 밴드는 한국에서뿐만 아니라 유럽에서도 인기 있다. (also, in Europe)

→ The band is popular _______________
_______________.

11 손님들이 도착하기 전에 우리는 집을 청소할 것이다. (the guests, arrive)

→ We will clean the house _______________
_______________.

12 내가 포기하지 않았기 때문에 그것을 할 수 있었다. (give up)

→ I was able to do it _______________
_______________.

13 너는 그가 초콜릿을 좋아한다는 것을 아니? (know, chocolate)

→ Do you _______________?

14 식물은 성장하기 위해 햇빛과 물 둘 다 필요로 한다. (sunlight, water)

→ Plants need _______________
to grow.

집중 훈련 3 통문장 영작하기
주어진 말을 활용하여 영작하시오.

15 나는 어렸을 때 중국에 살았다. (young, in China)

→ ___________________________

16 그녀는 산책을 하는 동안 길을 잃었다.
(get lost, take a walk)

→ ___________________________

17 문제는 그녀가 솔직하지 않다는 것이다.
(the problem, honest)

→ ___________________________

18 그녀가 우리 팀에 들어온다면, 나는 행복할 것이다.
(join our team, happy)

→ ___________________________

19 그녀 또는 나 둘 중 한 명이 저녁을 요리해야 한다.
(have to, cook)

→ ___________________________

20
A Can you help me this afternoon?
B 내가 바쁘지 않으면 내가 너를 도와줄게.
(unless, busy)

→ ___________________________

21
A Which does she like better, pizza or fried chicken?
B 그녀는 피자도 프라이드치킨도 좋아하지 않아.
(neither)

→ ___________________________

집중 훈련 4 조건 영작하기
우리말과 의미가 같도록 〈조건〉에 맞게 영작하시오.

22 우리는 수영하러 가거나 농구를 할 것이다.

조건 1 주어진 말을 모두 사용할 것
(will, go swimming, play basketball)
2 8단어로 쓸 것

→ ___________________________

23 그녀는 등산뿐만 아니라 캠핑도 무척 좋아한다.

조건 1 주어진 말을 활용할 것
(hiking, camping, love)
2 as를 포함한 문장으로 쓸 것
3 7단어의 문장으로 쓸 것

→ ___________________________

24 우리가 경기에 패배했다는 것은 충격적이었다.

조건 1 괄호 안에 주어진 말을 활용할 것
(it, lose the game, shocking)
2 과거시제 문장으로 쓸 것
3 모두 8단어로 쓸 것

→ ___________________________

25 이것은 영화가 아니라 연극이다.

조건 1 a movie와 a play를 사용할 것
2 총 8단어의 문장으로 쓸 것

→ ___________________________

서술형 **1**   (6점, 각 3점)

그림을 보고, 〈보기〉에서 알맞은 말을 골라 문장을 완성하시오. (한 번씩만 쓸 것)

보기	rings	computer games	when
	because	played	the doorbell

(1)

→ ___________ ___________ ___________
___________, the dog begins to bark.

(2)

→ She was sleepy ___________ ___________
___________ ___________ ___________ until
late.

서술형 **2**   (9점, 각 3점)

(A)와 (B)에 주어진 말을 <u>한 번씩</u> 사용하여 문장을 완성하시오.

(A)	(B)
while	· he didn't reply
but	· the rain stopped
after	· you're crossing the street

(1) We saw a rainbow ___________________
___________________.

(2) I sent John a text message, _____________
___________________.

(3) Don't use your phone ________________
___________________.

서술형 **3**   (4점)

우리말과 의미가 같도록 〈조건〉에 맞게 영작하시오.

> 네가 최선을 다하면 좋은 성적을 받을 것이다.

> 조건 **1** 주어진 말을 활용하시오.
> (do one's best, get a good grade)
> **2** 접속사로 문장을 시작하시오.
> **3** 11단어의 문장으로 서술하시오.

→ _______________________________

서술형 **4**   (3점)

알맞은 접속사를 사용하여 두 문장을 한 문장으로 쓰시오.

> I didn't know. The library is closed on Sundays.

→ _______________________________

서술형 **5** NEW   (8점, 각 2점)

Lisa의 가족들이 휴가에서 한 일을 보고, 〈보기〉에서 알맞은 접속사를 골라 문장을 완성하시오.

Lisa	built a sandcastle at the beach
Mike	played with a ball at the beach
Dad	got a massage, went to a café
Mom	took a walk in the park, went to a café

보기	not A but B	B as well as A
	both A and B	neither A nor B

(1) Dad ______________ Mom went to a café.

(2) __________ Mom __________ Dad got a
massage.

(3) __________ Mom __________ Dad went to
the beach.

(4) __________ Lisa __________ Mike spent time
at the beach.

10

관계대명사

1 주격 관계대명사 who

A 관계대명사는 두 문장을 연결하는 접속사와 대명사의 역할을 동시에 한다. 관계대명사가 이끄는 절은 앞에 나온 명사인 선행사를 뒤에서 꾸며 준다.

I like *the player*. + **He** scored three points.　나는 그 선수를 좋아한다. + 그가 3점을 득점했다.
↓
I like *the player* **who** scored three points.　나는 3점을 득점한 그 선수를 좋아한다.
　　　　　선행사　　　관계대명사

B 선행사가 사람이고, 관계대명사절에서 관계대명사가 주어 역할을 할 때 주격 관계대명사 who(that)을 쓴다.

| 주격 관계대명사 who | I know *an American* **who**(**that**) speaks Korean very well.
(← **She**(= The American) speaks Korean very well.) |

주의 관계대명사절의 동사는 관계대명사 앞에 있는 선행사의 인칭과 수에 일치시킨다.

I have *many friends* **who** **like** basketball.
　　　　선행사

1 주격 관계대명사절 의미 익히기

e.g. someone who has a car　→　_자동차를 가지고 있는 누군가_

1 the kid who was behind the tree　→　___________________

2 people who play tennis　→　___________________

3 the woman that travels a lot　→　___________________

4 the girl that is wearing a dress　→　___________________

2 주격 관계대명사 사용하여 문장 연결하기

1 I have a friend. He lives in Sydney.

→ I have a friend ___________________.

2 The boys are my cousins. They are swimming in the pool.

→ The boys ___________________ are my cousins.

3 She is an actress. She is popular in China.

→ She is an actress ___________________.

선행사가 사람이고, 관계대명사절에서 관계대명사가 목적어 역할을 할 때 목적격 관계대명사 whom〔who/that〕을 쓴다.

목적격 관계대명사 whom	He is *the actor* **whom**〔**who/that**〕I like. (← I like **him** (= the actor).)

TIP 목적격 관계대명사는 생략 가능하며, 구어체에서는 whom보다는 주로 who나 that을 쓴다.

The actor (**that**) I like will visit Korea tomorrow.

주의 관계대명사절의 수식을 받아 주어가 길어진 경우, 문장의 동사를 찾는 데 주의한다.

The woman **who(m)** I met yesterday **is** a lawyer.
주어　　　관계대명사절　　동사

1 목적격 관계대명사절 의미 익히기

e.g. the person whom I love the most → *내가 가장 사랑하는 사람*

1 the children who I want to meet → ______________________________

2 the woman that he married → ______________________________

3 people whom I know → ______________________________

4 the doctor that she visited → ______________________________

2 목적격 관계대명사 사용하여 문장 연결하기

1 They are classmates. I trust them completely.

→ They are classmates ___________ ___________ ___________ completely.

2 He is an artist. She met him in Greece.

→ He is the artist ___________ ___________ ___________ in Greece.

3 The singer will come here tonight. You like her.

→ The singer ___________ ___________ ___________ will come here tonight.

4 Mr. Brown is a teacher. I respect him most.

→ Mr. Brown is the teacher ___________ ___________ ___________ most.

5 The boy is in the hospital now. The truck hit the boy.

→ The boy ___________ ___________ ___________ ___________ is in the hospital now.

영작 기본 훈련

STEP 1 관계대명사 사용하여 의미 **확장하기** (관계대명사 that을 제외하고 쓸 것)

e.g.
ⓐ 그 소년은 이야기하고 있다.
The boy is talking.

ⓑ 나는 **이야기하고 있는** 소년을 안다.
I know the boy ___who___ ___is___ ___talking___ .

1
ⓐ 그 선수는 금메달을 땄다.
The player won the gold medal.

ⓑ **금메달을 딴** 선수는 내 아들이다.
The player _________ _________ the gold medal is my son.

2
ⓐ 나는 사람을 그렸다.
I drew a person.

ⓑ **내가 그린** 사람은 내 여동생이다.
The person _________ _________ _________ is my sister.

3
ⓐ 그 작가가 그 책을 썼다.
The author wrote the book.

ⓑ Brown 씨는 **그 책을 쓴** 작가이다.
Mr. Brown is the author _________ _________ the book.

4
ⓐ 그들은 그 아이를 발견했다.
They found the kid.

ⓑ **그들이 발견한** 아이는 Joe였다.
The kid _________ _________ _________ was Joe.

5
ⓐ 그 사람이 내 발을 밟았다.
The person stepped on my foot.

ⓑ 나는 **내 발을 밟은** 사람을 쳐다봤다.
I looked at the person _________ _________ on my foot.

6
ⓐ Sandy는 어제 그 남자를 만났다.
Sandy met the man yesterday.

ⓑ **Sandy가 어제 만난** 남자는 누구니?
Who is the man _________ _________ _________ yesterday?

7
ⓐ 그 소년은 안경을 끼고 있다.
The boy is wearing glasses.

ⓑ **안경을 끼고 있는** 소년은 내 사촌이다.
The boy _________ _________ _________ glasses is my cousin.

STEP **2** 영작 완성하기

1 그들은 몇 시간 동안 기다렸던 팬들이었다. (wait)

→ They were fans ___________ ___________ for hours.

2 Andrew는 내가 어젯밤에 전화한 친구이다. (call)

→ Andrew is the friend ___________ ___________ ___________ last night.

3 나는 이 문제를 해결할 수 있는 누군가가 필요하다. (solve)

→ I need someone ___________ ___________ ___________ this problem.

4 네가 도와드렸던 어르신은 Jake의 할아버지이다. (help)

→ The elderly man ___________ ___________ ___________ is Jake's grandfather.

5 군중에게 손을 흔들고 있는 남자는 영화배우이다. (wave)

→ The man ___________ ___________ ___________ to the crowd is a movie star.

STEP **3** 배열 영작하기

1 나는 나의 삼촌처럼 생긴 남자를 보았다. looked like, who, my uncle, a man

→ I saw ____.

2 내가 가르쳤던 그 학생은 똑똑했다. taught, the student, I, whom

→ ____ was smart.

3 우리는 무대 위에서 노래하고 있는 소녀를 안다. singing, the girl, is, on the stage, who

→ We know ____.

4 그는 우리가 초대한 사람이 아니었다. that, invited, we, a person

→ He was not ____.

5 2층에 사는 여자는 일본인이다. who, the woman, on the second floor, lives

→ ____ is Japanese.

선행사가 사물이나 동물인 경우에는 관계대명사 which〔that〕을 쓰며, 주격과 목적격의 형태가 같다.

주격 관계대명사 which	Lucy likes *books* **which**〔**that**〕 have many pictures. (← **They**(= The books) have many pictures.)
목적격 관계대명사 which	Peter found *the umbrella* **which**〔**that**〕 he lost the other day. (← He lost **it**(= the umbrella) the other day.)

주의 목적격 관계대명사가 관계대명사절에서 목적어 역할을 하므로 목적어를 또 쓰지 않도록 주의한다.

Peter found the umbrella **which**〔**that**〕 he lost it. (×)

TIP 목적격 관계대명사 which〔that〕은 생략할 수 있다.

I like the bike (**which**〔**that**〕) he bought for me.

1 주격 관계대명사 사용하여 문장 연결하기

1 Sarah has a bag. It has many pockets.

→ Sarah has a bag ____________ ____________ many pockets.

2 The store is closed today. It sells accessories.

→ The store ____________ ____________ accessories is closed today.

3 She picked up the magazines. They were on the sofa.

→ She picked up the magazines ____________ ____________ on the sofa.

4 The building is a museum. It looks like a mushroom.

→ The building ____________ ____________ like a mushroom is a museum.

2 목적격 관계대명사 사용하여 문장 연결하기

1 This is the cup. I use it every day.

→ This is the cup ____________ ____________ ____________ every day.

2 The backpack looks very heavy. He is carrying it.

→ The backpack ____________ ____________ ____________ ____________ looks very heavy.

3 The poems were wonderful. I learned them at school.

→ The poems ____________ ____________ ____________ at school were wonderful.

 4 소유격 관계대명사 whose

관계대명사절에서 관계대명사가 소유격 역할을 할 때, 선행사의 종류에 관계없이 소유격 관계대명사 whose를 쓴다.

I have *a friend*. + **His** sister lives in France.　나에게는 친구가 있다. + 그의 누나는 프랑스에 산다.

↓

I have *a friend* **whose** sister lives in France.　나에게는 누나가 프랑스에 사는 친구가 있다.

> **TIP**　소유격 관계대명사 whose 뒤에는 반드시 명사가 온다.
>
> I know *a girl* **whose** mother works at a library.　(소녀의 어머니가 도서관에서 일함)
> They live in *a city* **whose** streets are not crowded.　(도시의 거리들이 붐비지 않음)

1 소유격 관계대명사절 의미 익히기

e.g.　a cat whose tail is long　→　꼬리가 긴 고양이

1　a boy whose eyes are beautiful　→ ______________________________

2　a bike whose wheels are big　→ ______________________________

3　the car whose door is broken　→ ______________________________

4　the movie whose title is too long　→ ______________________________

2 소유격 관계대명사 사용하여 문장 연결하기

1　I joined an orchestra. Its members were all students.

→ I joined an orchestra ___________ ___________ ___________ all students.

2　The phone is popular. Its screen is wide.

→ The phone ___________ ___________ ___________ wide is popular.

3　Amy has a brother. His hobby is watching the stars.

→ Amy has a brother ___________ ___________ ___________ watching the stars.

4　We work at a company. Its workers are friendly.

→ We work at a company ___________ ___________ ___________ friendly.

5　The dogs walk very fast. Their legs are short.

→ The dogs ___________ ___________ ___________ short walk very fast.

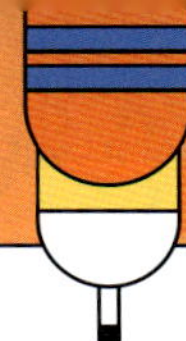

영작 기본 훈련

STEP 1 관계대명사 사용하여 의미 **확장하기**

e.g.
a 그 소녀의 이름은 Lucy이다. — The girl's name is Lucy.
b **이름이 Lucy인** 소녀를 찾아라. — Find the girl _whose_ _name_ _is_ _Lucy_ .

1
a 한 가게가 양초를 판다. — A store sells candles.
b 그곳은 **양초를 파는** 가게이다. — It's a store __________ __________ __________ .

2
a 그녀가 그 쿠키들을 구웠다. — She baked the cookies.
b **그녀가 구운** 쿠키들은 맛있다. — The cookies __________ __________ __________ are delicious.

3
a 그 소년의 아버지는 은행에서 일하신다. — The boy's father works at a bank.
b 그는 **아버지가 은행에서 일하시는** 소년이다. — He is the boy __________ __________ __________ at a bank.

4
a 그는 나에게 야구 모자를 사 줬다. — He bought me a cap.
b 나는 **그가 내게 사 준** 야구 모자를 좋아한다. — I like the cap __________ __________ __________ me.

5
a 그 방은 바다 전망이다. — The room has an ocean view.
b 나는 **바다 전망인** 방을 원한다. — I want a room __________ __________ an ocean view.

6
a 내 엄마가 그 꽃병을 만드셨다. — My mom made the vase.
b 내 누나는 **엄마가 만드신** 꽃병을 깼다. — My sister broke the vase __________ __________ __________ .

7
a 그 노래들은 요즘 인기 있다. — The songs are popular these days.
b 우리는 **요즘 인기 있는** 노래들을 불렀다. — We sang songs __________ __________ __________ these days.

STEP **2** 영작 완성하기

1 너는 네가 잃어버린 열쇠를 찾았니? (the key, lose)

→ Did you find ___________ ___________ ___________ ___________ ___________?

2 그녀는 내게 자판이 망가진 노트북을 빌려주었다. (a laptop, keyboard)

→ She lent me ___________ ___________ ___________ ___________ was broken.

3 나는 빨리 마르는 셔츠를 찾고 있다. (dry, quickly)

→ I'm looking for a shirt ___________ ___________ ___________.

4 나는 줄거리가 단순한 소설을 좋아한다. (storylines, be simple)

→ I like novels ___________ ___________ ___________ ___________.

5 우리가 먹은 음식은 맛있었다. (the food, eat)

→ ___________ ___________ ___________ ___________ was tasty.

STEP **3** 배열 영작하기

1 Tony가 쓴 이야기는 우주에 관한 것이었다.   Tony, space, wrote, was, about, that

→ The story ____.

2 Jane은 귀가 큰 고양이 한 마리를 키운다.   a cat, has, big, are, whose, ears

→ Jane ____.

3 나는 언니가 경찰인 친구가 한 명 있다.   a friend, is, whose, have, a police officer, sister, I

→ ____

4 그들이 방문한 건물은 오랜 역사를 가지고 있다.   has, visited, they, the building, a long history

→ ____

5 그 식당은 제철인 채소들을 사용한다.   uses, in season, the restaurant, are, vegetables, that

→ ____

관계대명사 that은 선행사의 종류에 관계없이 주격 또는 목적격 관계대명사로 쓸 수 있다.
다음과 같은 경우 주로 관계대명사 that을 쓴다.

선행사가 「사람+사물」일 때	I met *the man and the dog* **that** live next door.
선행사가 -thing, -body일 때	She said *something* **that** made me laugh.
선행사에 최상급이 있을 때	He was *the fastest runner* **that** I know.
선행사에 all, every, any, the only, the same, the very, 서수 등이 있을 때	This is *all the information* **that** I have. She was *the only person* **that** knew the secret.

1 관계대명사 that절 의미 익히기

e.g. everything that was on his plate → _그의 접시 위에 있던 모든 것_

1 the very boy that I met at the camp → ______________________

2 the best moment that I experienced → ______________________

3 the only student that answered the question → ______________________

2 관계대명사 that 형태 적용하기

1 이것은 내가 본 가장 큰 케이크이다. (big, cake)

→ This is __________ __________ __________ __________ I have ever seen.

2 그는 네가 산 것과 똑같은 시계를 갖고 있다. (same, watch)

→ He has __________ __________ __________ __________ you bought.

3 나를 이해하는 사람은 아무도 없다. (nobody)

→ There's __________ __________ understands me.

4 나는 그에게 내가 가진 모든 돈을 주었다. (all the money)

→ I gave him __________ __________ __________ __________ I had.

5 너는 내가 믿을 수 있는 유일한 친구이다. (only)

→ You are __________ __________ __________ __________ I can trust.

6 관계대명사 what

A 관계대명사 what은 '~하는 것'이라는 의미로 선행사를 포함한다. what이 이끄는 절은 명사절로, 문장 안에서 주어, 목적어, 보어 역할을 한다.

주어	**What** we need now isn't money.
목적어	Jack explained **what** he saw.
보어	These cups are **what** I made for my parents.

> what이 이끄는 관계대명사절이 주어로 쓰이면 단수 취급한다.
> **What** you heard **is** true.

B 관계대명사 that *vs.* 관계대명사 what

that (선행사 수식)	I like *the dress* **that** my mom bought for me.	엄마가 내게 사 주신 드레스
what (선행사 포함)	I like **what** my mom bought for me. (= *the thing* that)	엄마가 내게 사 주신 것

1 관계대명사 that과 what 쓰임 익히기

e.g.

그녀가 한 말	→ the words <u>that(which)</u> she said
그녀가 말한 것	→ ___ what ___ she ___ said ___

1 그가 만든 가방 → the bag ___________ he made

그가 만든 것 → ___________ ___________ ___________

2 내가 입고 있는 옷 → the clothes ___________ I'm wearing

내가 입고 있는 것 → ___________ ___________ ___________

2 관계대명사 what 형태 적용하기

1 내가 원하는 것은 새 운동화이다. (want)

→ ___________ ___________ ___________ is new sneakers.

2 네가 신문에서 읽은 것을 반 친구들에게 말해 주겠니? (read)

→ Will you tell your classmates ___________ ___________ ___________ in the newspaper?

3 그것이 바로 내가 믿는 것이다. (believe)

→ That's exactly ___________ ___________ ___________.

STEP 1 관계대명사 의미 **비교하기** (관계대명사 that 또는 what을 사용할 것)

1 write

ⓐ 이것이 **그가 쓴 것**이다.
This is __________ __________ __________.

ⓑ 이것이 **그가 쓴** 바로 그 시이다.
This is the very poem __________ __________ __________.

2 draw

ⓐ **네가 그린** 그림은 아름답다.
The picture __________ __________ __________ is beautiful.

ⓑ **네가 그린 것**은 아름답다.
__________ __________ __________ is beautiful.

3 build

ⓐ 나는 **그들이 지은 것**을 봤다.
I saw __________ __________ __________.

ⓑ 나는 **그들이 지은** 건물들을 봤다.
I saw the buildings __________ __________ __________.

4 cook

ⓐ **그가 요리한 것**은 맛이 좋았다.
__________ __________ __________ tasted good.

ⓑ **그가 요리한** 음식은 맛이 좋았다.
The food __________ __________ __________ tasted good.

5 want

ⓐ 나는 **내가 원했던** 모든 것을 샀다.
I bought everything __________ __________ __________.

ⓑ 나는 **내가 원했던 것**을 샀다.
I bought __________ __________ __________.

6 say

ⓐ 나는 **그가 말한 것들**을 듣지 못했다.
I didn't hear the things __________ __________ __________.

ⓑ 나는 **그가 말한 것**을 듣지 못했다.
I didn't hear __________ __________ __________.

7 do

ⓐ **네가 한 것**은 놀랍다.
__________ __________ __________ is amazing.

ⓑ **네가 한** 일은 놀랍다.
The work __________ __________ __________ is amazing.

8 make

ⓐ 이것은 **그가 만든 것**이다.
This is __________ __________ __________.

ⓑ 이것은 **그가 만든** 첫 번째 의자이다.
This is the first chair __________ __________ __________.

STEP **2** 영작 **완성하기**

1 너의 대답은 내가 기대했던 것이 아니었다. (expect)

→ Your answer was not __________ __________ __________.

2 우리가 너를 위해 할 수 있는 무언가가 있니? (anything, do)

→ Is there __________ __________ __________ __________ __________ for you?

3 여러분이 필요한 것을 제게 말해 주세요. (tell, need)

→ Please __________ __________ __________ __________ __________.

4 이것이 나를 울게 한 유일한 영화이다. (movie, make)

→ This is __________ __________ __________ __________ __________ me cry.

5 그들이 판매하는 것은 가장 좋은 상품이다. (sell)

→ __________ __________ __________ __________ the best product.

STEP **3** 배열 **영작하기**

1 그 아이는 크리스마스에 그가 받은 모든 선물들을 열어 보았다. the child, got, all the presents, that, opened, he

→ _________________________________ on Christmas.

2 그 사건의 진실은 사람들이 믿던 것과 달랐다. people, was, from, believed, different, what

→ The truth of the accident _________________________________.

3 우리는 Dan이 태어났던 바로 그 집을 방문했다. Dan, that, house, the very, was born in

→ We visited _________________________________.

4 선생님은 우리가 쓴 것을 확인하셨다. checked, we, what, wrote, the teacher

→ _________________________________

5 달리고 있는 소녀와 개를 봐. look at, running, and, the girl, are, the dog, that

→ _________________________________

집중 훈련 1 틀린 부분 고치기
어법상 **틀린** 부분을 찾아 바르게 고치시오.

집중 훈련 2 영작 완성하기 (관계대명사를 사용할 것)
주어진 말을 활용하여 문장을 완성하시오.

01 She is the person which won first prize.
그녀가 일등상을 탄 사람이다.

_________ → _________

02 This is the watch who John gave me.
이것은 John이 내게 준 손목시계이다.

_________ → _________

03 Do you know the girl who mom is a nurse?
너는 엄마가 간호사이신 그 소녀를 아니?

_________ → _________

04 That you said is hard to believe.
네가 말한 것은 믿기 어렵다.

_________ → _________

05 He knows two girls who likes baseball.
그는 야구를 좋아하는 두 명의 소녀를 알고 있다.

_________ → _________

06 Our English teacher is a person which everyone likes.
우리 영어 선생님은 모두가 좋아하는 사람이다.

_________ → _________

07 I saw the boy and the dog which were taking a walk together.
나는 함께 산책하고 있던 소년과 개를 보았다.

_________ → _________

08 Woods 씨가 이 그림을 그린 화가이다.
(paint, this picture)

→ Ms. Woods is the artist _________ _________.

09 그들은 많은 어린이들이 존경하는 우주 비행사들이다.
(many children, admire)

→ They are astronauts _________ _________.

10 그 축제에서 우리가 본 것을 너에게 말해 줄게. (see)

→ We'll tell you _________ at the festival.

11 이것이 내가 너에게 줄 수 있는 마지막 충고이다.
(the last, advice)

→ This is _________ I can give you.

12 나는 생각이 독특한 몇몇 사람들을 만났다.
(some people, ideas)

→ I met _________ were unique.

13 그 도둑이 훔친 것은 비싼 목걸이였다. (the thief, steal)

→ _________ was an expensive necklace.

14 너는 그 시험에 합격한 유일한 사람이다.
(the only, pass)

→ You are _________ the test.

집중 훈련 3 **통문장 영작하기** (관계대명사를 사용할 것)
주어진 말을 활용하여 영작하시오.

15 나는 어제 산 그 책을 읽었다. (buy)

→ __________________________________

16 이것이 내가 주문한 바로 그 음식이다. (the very, order)

→ __________________________________

17 나는 나에게 말을 했던 그 남자를 모른다.
(know, talk to me)

→ __________________________________

18 그는 신발을 만드는 회사에서 일한다.
(work for a company)

→ __________________________________

19 나는 취미가 피겨 스케이팅인 한 친구가 있다.
(hobby, figure skating)

→ __________________________________

20

A Did you get a good grade on your math test?
B No. 그것은 내가 올해 받은 최악의 성적이야.
(the worst grade, get, this year)

→ __________________________________

21

A I had a fantastic weekend. I went to Jeju Island.
B That sounds fun!
그곳에서 네가 찍은 사진들을 내게 보여 줘.
(take, the pictures, there)

→ __________________________________

집중 훈련 4 **조건 영작하기**
우리말과 의미가 같도록 〈조건〉에 맞게 영작하시오.

22 나는 Amy가 보낸 이메일을 받았다.

조건 1 주어진 말을 활용할 것
(send, get, the email)
2 관계대명사를 포함할 것
3 7단어의 문장으로 쓸 것

→ __________________________________

23 그는 그녀가 말한 것을 기억할 수 없었다.

조건 1 괄호 안에 주어진 말을 활용할 것
(couldn't, remember, say)
2 모두 6단어로 쓸 것

→ __________________________________

24 나는 아침에 일찍 일어나는 사람들을 존경한다.

조건 1 〈보기〉에 있는 말을 모두 사용할 것
2 who, whom, which 중에서 알맞은 것을
골라 쓸 것

보기 people   respect   wake up
early in the morning

→ __________________________________

25 나는 네가 알고 있는 모든 것을 알고 싶다.

조건 1 관계대명사를 반드시 포함할 것
2 want, know, everything을 사용할 것
(필요한 경우 두 번 사용할 것)
3 총 8단어의 문장으로 쓸 것

→ __________________________________

서술형 **1** (4점)

그림을 보고, 〈조건〉에 맞게 문장을 완성하시오.

조건　**1**　관계대명사를 반드시 사용하시오.
　　　2　주어진 말을 활용하시오. (the gift, give)

→　My father liked ___________ __________
　　__________ we __________ him.

서술형 **2** (4점)

우리말과 의미가 같도록 〈조건〉에 맞게 영작하시오.

한국 드라마를 좋아하는 관광객들이 이 장소를 방문할 것이다.

조건　**1**　관계대명사를 사용하시오.
　　　2　주어진 말을 사용하시오.
　　　　　(tourists, Korean dramas, this place)
　　　3　9단어의 문장으로 서술하시오.

→　______________________________
　　______________________________

서술형 **3** (4점)

알맞은 관계대명사를 사용하여 두 문장을 한 문장으로 쓰시오.

Look at the house. Its roof is white.

→　______________________________

서술형 **4** (9점, 각 3점)

우리말과 의미가 같도록 (A)와 (B)에 주어진 말을 <u>한 번씩</u> 활용하여 문장을 완성하시오.

(A)	(B)
who	· be wearing
that	· hair is long
whose	· be standing behind you

(1) 이것이 Kate가 입고 있던 것과 같은 티셔츠이다.

→　This is the same T-shirt _______________
　　__________.

(2) 네 뒤에 서 있던 여자는 나의 이모이다.

→　The woman _____________________
　　is my aunt.

(3) 나는 털이 긴 개를 키운다.

→　I have a dog _____________________.

서술형 **5** NEW (9점, 각 3점)

다음 대화를 읽고, 물음에 답하시오.

Cindy ⓐ Did you see the movie? It is playing now at Star Cinema.
David No, not yet. Do you want to see it?
Cindy No. ⓑ 네가 보고 싶은 것을 내게 말해 봐.
David I'd like to see ⓒ (that, saw, Amy, the horror movie) last Sunday.

(1) 관계대명사 that을 사용하여 ⓐ를 한 문장으로 쓰시오.

→　Did you see the movie _______________
　　______________________?

(2) 알맞은 관계대명사를 사용하여 밑줄 친 ⓑ를 영작하시오. (5단어로 쓸 것)

→　Tell me _____________________.

(3) 자연스러운 문장이 되도록 ⓒ에 주어진 단어들을 알맞게 배열하시오.

→　______________________________

동아출판 영어 교재 가이드

중학 문법＋쓰기

클리어.

Level **2**

Answers

동아출판

중학 문법+쓰기

클리어.

Level 2

Answers

chapter **1** 시제

1 현재시제와 과거시제   p. 8

1 1 I studied.   2 You slept.   3 We ran.
   4 She danced.   5 They went.   6 Bill tried.
   7 The leaves fell.
2 1 lived / live   2 teaches / taught   3 ate / eat

2 현재진행형과 과거진행형   p. 9

1 1 is sleeping / was sleeping
   2 are watching / were watching
   3 is snowing / was snowing
   4 are running / were running
2 1 are climbing   2 was sitting   3 am baking
   4 were studying

영작 기본 훈련   pp. 10~11

STEP 1

1 ⓐ took   ⓑ takes
2 ⓐ boils   ⓑ is boiling
3 ⓐ rang   ⓑ was ringing
4 ⓐ holds   ⓑ held
5 ⓐ am exercising   ⓑ was exercising
6 ⓐ rose   ⓑ is rising
7 ⓐ plays   ⓑ is playing
8 ⓐ got up   ⓑ get up

STEP 2

1 opens   2 were staying
3 arrived   4 is doing
5 know   6 bought

STEP 3

1 Larry plays badminton with his friends
2 The man was fixing a car
3 I am(I'm) setting the table
4 They went to the amusement park

3 미래시제   p. 12

1 1 We will jump. / We are going to jump.
   2 I will sleep. / I am going to sleep.
   3 She will sing. / She is going to sing.
   4 They will swim. / They are going to swim.
2 1 will ride   2 is going to be
   3 am going to eat   4 will invite

4 미래시제의 부정문과 의문문   p. 13

1 1 will not finish / Will they finish
   2 are not going to take / Are we going to take
   3 isn't going to wear / Is she going to wear
   4 won't clean / Will he clean
   5 aren't going to go / Are you going to go

영작 기본 훈련   pp. 14~15

STEP 1

1 ⓐ meets   ⓑ will not meet   ⓒ Will she meet
2 ⓐ jogs   ⓑ is going to jog
   ⓒ is not going to jog
3 ⓐ take   ⓑ are going to take
   ⓒ Are they going to take
4 ⓐ snows   ⓑ won't snow   ⓒ Will it snow
5 ⓐ order   ⓑ are going to order
   ⓒ Are we going to order
6 ⓐ do   ⓑ going to do   ⓒ I'm not going to do

STEP 2

1 are not going to play   2 Will he practice
3 won't buy   4 Is Susan going to go

STEP 3

1 It will not rain
2 Will you go to that restaurant
3 He is not going to change his phone number.
4 We will prepare for the festival.
5 Is your family going to move to a new house?

1 1 have bought　2 have read　3 have played
4 have eaten　5 have gone　6 have been
7 have written
2 1 have seen / have not (never) seen
2 have stayed / Have, stayed
3 has, met / Has, met

1 1 has studied　2 have never seen
3 has, arrived　4 have known
5 has not started　6 Have, tried
7 has, finished　8 Have, visited

영작 기본 훈련　pp. 18~19

STEP 1

1　ⓐ did　　ⓑ have, done
2　ⓐ worked　　ⓑ has worked
3　ⓐ didn't call　　ⓑ has not called
4　ⓐ did, read　　ⓑ Have, read
5　ⓐ lost　　ⓑ has lost
6　ⓐ didn't meet　　ⓑ have, met
7　ⓐ were　　ⓑ have been
8　ⓐ Did, leave　　ⓑ Has, left

STEP 2

1　has lived　　　　2　has, changed
3　has, passed　　　4　has gone

STEP 3

1　has been sick since last Saturday
2　They have not returned from the trip
3　Have you ever seen a magic show?
4　I have played the guitar for five months.
5　She has never eaten Mexican food before.

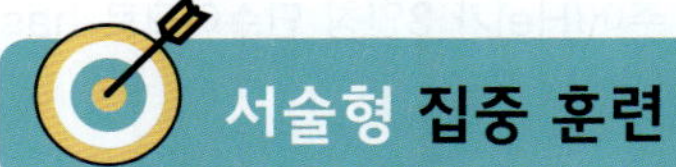

서술형 집중 훈련　pp. 20~21

집중 훈련 1

01 begins → began　　02 buying → buy
03 am knowing → know　　04 had → have had
05 washing → are washing
06 will do not → will not (won't) do
07 saw → has seen

집중 훈련 2

08 was not (wasn't) listening
09 am going to return　　10 has gone
11 brushes his teeth　　12 have you stayed
13 will not (won't) pass　　14 has already sent

집중 훈련 3

15 Emma has four puppies.
16 They have worked there for two years.
17 Tom was drawing a picture an (one) hour ago.
18 Are you going to leave Seoul next month?
19 Jane rode her bike yesterday.
20 Will you call him tomorrow?
21 Has he been to Europe?

집중 훈련 4

22 She isn't going to study math tomorrow.
23 John has never seen the Eiffel Tower.
24 Joe and Amy were looking for their dog.
25 Julie reads the newspaper every morning.

01 과거를 나타내는 last weekend가 있으므로 과거시제(began)
로 쓴다.
02 미래시제 의문문은 「Be동사＋주어＋going to＋동사원형 ~?」
이므로 to 뒤에는 동사원형(buy)을 쓴다.
03 인식을 나타내는 동사는 진행형으로 쓰지 않으므로 현재시제
(know)로 쓴다.
04 과거부터 현재까지 계속되는 일을 나타내므로 현재완료 「have/
has＋p.p.」 형태로 쓴다.
05 지금 일어나고 있는 일을 나타내므로 현재진행형 「be동사의 현
재형＋-ing」로 쓴다.
06 미래시제 부정문은 「will not (won't)＋동사원형」으로 쓴다.
07 과거부터 현재까지의 경험을 나타내므로 현재완료 「have/

has+p.p.」 형태로 쓴다. 주어(He)가 3인칭 단수이므로 has
seen으로 쓴다.

08 '~하고 있지 않았다'라는 의미의 과거진행형 부정문은 「be동사
의 과거형+not+-ing」로 쓴다.

09 going을 사용한 미래시제는 「be going to+동사원형」으로 쓴
다.

10 과거에 인도에 가서 지금 여기에 없는 결과를 나타내므로 현재완
료 「have/has+p.p.」 형태로 쓴다. 주어(Sam)가 3인칭 단수
이므로 has gone으로 쓴다.

11 현재의 습관을 나타내므로 현재시제로 쓴다. -sh로 끝나는 동사
는 주어가 3인칭 단수일 때 -es를 붙인다.

12 과거부터 현재까지 계속되는 일을 나타내므로 현재완료 의문문
「Have/Has+주어+p.p. ~?」 형태로 쓴다.

13 will을 사용한 미래시제 부정문은 「will not〔won't〕+동사원형」
으로 쓴다.

14 이미 완료된 일을 나타내므로 현재완료 「have/has+p.p.」 형
태로 쓴다. 주어(Sally)가 3인칭 단수이므로 has sent로 쓴다.
부사 already는 보통 have와 p.p. 사이에 쓴다.

15 동사 have가 소유를 나타낼 때는 진행형으로 쓰지 않는다. 주어
(Emma)가 3인칭 단수이고 현재시제이므로 has로 쓴다.

16 과거부터 현재까지 계속되는 일을 나타내므로 현재완료 「have/
has+p.p.」 형태로 쓴다.

17 '~하고 있었다'라는 의미의 과거진행형은 「be동사의 과거형
+-ing」로 쓴다.

18 going을 사용한 미래시제 의문문은 「Be동사+주어+going
to+동사원형 ~?」으로 쓴다.

19 어제(yesterday) 일어난 일이므로 과거시제로 쓴다. ride의 과
거형은 rode이다.

20 will을 사용한 미래시제 의문문은 「Will+주어+동사원형 ~?」으
로 쓴다.

21 과거부터 현재까지의 경험을 나타내므로 현재완료 의문문
「Have/Has+주어+p.p. ~?」 형태로 쓴다.

22 going을 사용한 미래시제 부정문은 「be동사+not+going
to+동사원형」으로 쓴다. 주어가 she이므로 be동사는 is를 쓰
며, 부정 표현은 줄여 쓰라는 조건에 맞게 isn't로 쓴다.

23 과거부터 현재까지의 경험을 나타내므로 현재완료 부정문
「have/has+not〔never〕+p.p.」 형태로 쓴다. 주어(John)가
3인칭 단수이므로 has never seen으로 쓴다.

24 '~하고 있었다'라는 의미의 과거진행형은 「be동사의 과거형
+-ing」로 쓴다. 주어(Joe and Amy)가 복수이므로 be동사는
were를 쓴다.

25 현재의 습관은 현재시제로 쓴다. 주어(Julie)가 3인칭 단수이므
로 동사에 -s를 붙인다.

1 (1) Chris has not〔hasn't〕 planned his vacation
　　(2) Is Chris going to visit his grandparents?
2 (1) will watch　(2) were waiting for me
3 (1) went to the beach　(2) is making sandwiches
4 (1) arrived　(2) Has, taught　(3) have, heard
5 is having → has
6 (1) is going to eat out　(2) are going to go
　　(3) will take a walk

1 (1) 현재완료 부정문은 「have/has+not+p.p.」로 쓴다.
　　(2) be going to를 사용한 미래시제 의문문은 「Be동사+주어
　　+going to+동사원형 ~?」으로 쓴다.
2 (1) 미래의 일을 말하고 있으므로 「will+동사원형」으로 쓴다.
　　(2) '~하고 있었다'라는 의미의 과거진행형인 「be동사의 과거형
　　+-ing」로 쓴다.
3 (1) 과거를 나타내는 yesterday가 있으므로 과거시제로 쓴다.
　　(2) 지금 하고 있는 일은 현재진행형으로 나타낸다.
4 (1) 과거를 나타내는 an hour ago가 있으므로 과거시제로 쓴
　　다.
　　(2) since가 '~ 이후로'라는 계속의 의미를 나타내므로 현재완료
　　의문문 「Have/Has+주어+p.p. ~?」 형태로 쓴다.
　　(3) never와 before가 함께 쓰여 과거부터 현재까지의 경험을
　　나타내므로 현재완료로 쓴다
5 동사 have가 소유를 나타낼 때는 진행형으로 쓰지 않는다. 주어
　　(Sarah)가 3인칭 단수이므로 has로 쓴다.
6 (1) 주어(Tom)가 3인칭 단수이므로 be동사는 is를 쓴다.
　　(2) 주어(Tom and Joe)가 복수이므로 be동사는 are를 쓴다.
　　(3) 미래를 나타내는 will은 주어와 상관없이 「will+동사원형」을
　　쓴다.

chapter ❷ 조동사

❶ can, may
p. 24

1 **1** can / cannot(can't) swim
  2 may / may not come
2 **1** May, turn   **2** Can, pass   **3** can't be
  4 am able to solve

❷ must, have to
p. 25

1 **1** must / must not eat
  2 have to / don't have to stand
  3 have to / must be
2 **1** must be   **2** has to help   **3** must not take
  4 had to paint

영작 기본 훈련
pp. 26~27

STEP ❶

1 ⓑ must not close   ⓒ don't have to close
2 ⓑ must be   ⓒ cannot(can't) be
3 ⓑ cannot(can't) move   ⓒ wasn't able to move
4 ⓑ May(Can), wait   ⓒ Can(Could), wait
5 ⓑ doesn't have to cook   ⓒ Does, have to cook
6 ⓑ had to go   ⓒ didn't have to go

STEP ❷

1 may lose   **2** must know
3 Can, finish   **4** cannot(can't) be
5 has to feed

STEP ❸

1 Students must not make noise
2 was able to repair the car
3 may not come back in two weeks
4 don't have to write a book report
5 May I use this computer?

❸ should, had better
p. 28

1 **1** 친절해야 한다   **2** 뛰면 안 된다
  3 멈추는 게 낫다〔좋겠다〕   **4** 떠나는 게 낫다〔좋겠다〕
  5 잊지 않는 게 낫다〔좋겠다〕
2 **1** should do   **2** had better not spread
  3 had better see   **4** should not run

❹ used to, would like to
p. 29

1 **1** exercised / used to exercise
  2 stay / would like to stay
2 **1** would like to join   **2** used to be
  3 used to take   **4** would like to ask

영작 기본 훈련
pp. 30~31

STEP ❶

1 ⓑ should(must) take   ⓒ had better take
2 ⓑ would like to play   ⓒ used to play
3 ⓑ had better change   ⓒ would like to change
4 ⓑ should(must) not stay   ⓒ had better not stay
5 ⓑ would like to bake   ⓒ would bake
6 ⓑ used to be   ⓒ must be

STEP ❷

1 should eat   **2** used to be
3 would like to drink   **4** would go
5 had better not lie

STEP ❸

1 should not pick flowers in the park
2 used to go to the same school
3 had better wear your seat belt
4 I would like to travel around Europe
5 You had better not call him

집중 훈련 1

01 comes → come
02 has → had
03 must not → do not(don't) have to
04 are → were (또는 are not able to → could not (couldn't))
05 can → must
06 was used to → used to(would)
07 May → Can(Could)

집중 훈련 2

08 I would(I'd) like to take
09 You must(may/should) not touch
10 used to be a police officer
11 had better(should) save some money
12 Can(May) I take a seat
13 had to come home
14 cannot(can't) be your book

집중 훈련 3

15 You can(may) go out for lunch.
16 He used to(would) go to the gym on Saturdays.
17 She must be Eric's mom.
18 He may not bring his laptop.
19 I would(I'd) like to rest under that tree.
20 Can(May) I talk to you now?
21 You don't have to finish it tonight.

집중 훈련 4

22 Henry has to sell his car.
23 They weren't able to speak Korean last year.
24 Jennifer doesn't have to go to school today.
25 You had better not eat anything before bed.

01 조동사 뒤에는 항상 동사원형을 쓴다.
02 '~하는 것이 좋겠다'라는 의미의 had better는 주어의 인칭이나 수에 관계없이 형태가 변하지 않는다.
03 '~할 필요가 없다'라는 의미는 don't have to를 써서 나타낸다.
04 '~할 수 없었다'라는 의미는 「was/were not able to+동사원형」 또는 「could not(couldn't)+동사원형」을 써서 나타낸다.

주어(We)가 복수이므로 were를 쓴다.
05 '~임이 틀림없다'라는 강한 추측을 나타낼 때는 must를 쓴다.
06 '~하곤 했다'라는 과거의 습관을 나타낼 때는 used to 또는 would를 쓴다.
07 '~해 주겠니/주시겠어요?'라는 요청을 나타낼 때는 Can you ~?를 쓴다. could를 쓰면 더욱 정중한 요청이 된다.
08 '~하고 싶다'라는 소망을 나타낼 때는 「would like to+동사원형」을 쓴다.
09 '~하면 안 된다'라는 금지를 나타낼 때는 must(may/should) not을 쓴다.
10 '~이었다'라는 과거의 상태를 나타낼 때는 used to를 쓴다.
11 '~하는 것이 좋겠다'라는 충고를 나타낼 때는 had better 또는 should를 쓴다.
12 '~해도 될까요?'라는 의미의 허가를 구하는 표현은 Can(May) I ~?를 쓴다.
13 must(have to)의 과거형은 had to를 쓴다.
14 '~일 리 없다'라는 강한 부정적 추측을 나타낼 때는 cannot (can't)를 쓴다.
15 '~해도 된다'라는 허가를 나타낼 때는 can 또는 may를 쓴다.
16 '~하곤 했다'라는 과거의 습관을 나타낼 때는 조동사 used to 또는 would를 쓴다.
17 '~임이 틀림없다'라는 강한 추측을 나타낼 때는 must를 쓴다.
18 '~하지 않을지도 모른다'라는 부정의 추측을 나타낼 때는 may not을 쓴다.
19 '~하고 싶다'라는 소망을 나타낼 때는 「would like to+동사원형」을 쓴다.
20 '~해도 될까요?'라는 의미의 허가를 구하는 표현은 Can(May) I ~?를 쓴다.
21 '~할 필요가 없다'라는 의미는 don't have to를 써서 나타낸다.
22 have를 이용해서 '~해야 한다'라는 의무를 나타낼 때는 have/has to를 쓴다. 주어(Henry)가 3인칭 단수이므로 has to를 쓴다.
23 '~할 수 없었다'라는 의미는 「was/were not able to+동사원형」을 써서 나타낸다. 주어(They)가 복수이므로 were를 쓴다.
24 '~할 필요가 없다'라는 의미는 don't/doesn't have to를 써서 나타낸다. 주어(Jennifer)가 3인칭 단수이므로 doesn't를 쓴다.
25 '~하지 않는 것이 좋겠다'라는 의미를 나타낼 때는 had better not 또는 should not을 쓴다. 글자 수 조건에 맞게 had better not을 쓴다.

CHAPTER 2

서술형 실전 TEST

1 (1) shouldn't skip (2) would like to watch
(3) must be (4) had better hurry
(5) used to take walks
2 (1) Can(Could) you lend
(2) We weren't able to(couldn't) buy tickets.
3 used to be
4 (1) That boy cannot be Danny.
(2) We must not waste time.
5 ② have to → do not(don't) have to

1 (1) ~하면 안 된다, ~하지 않는 것이 좋다: shouldn't
(2) ~하고 싶다: would like to
(3) ~임이 틀림없다: must
(4) ~하는 것이 좋겠다: had better
(5) ~하곤 했다: used to
2 (1) ~해 주겠니?: Can(Could) you ~?
(2) ~할 수 없었다: was/were not able to 또는 could not
(couldn't)
3 '~이었다'라는 과거의 상태를 나타낼 때는 used to를 쓴다.
4 (1) ~일 리가 없다: cannot
(2) ~하면 안 된다: must not
5 해석 **Betty** 콘서트는 몇 시에 시작하니?
Joe 7시 30분에 시작해.
Betty 우리가 거기에 7시 전에 가야 하니?
Joe 그럴 필요 없어. 7시 15분까지는 가야 해.
Betty 알았어. 카메라를 가져가도 될까?
Joe 물론이지. 하지만 콘서트 동안에는 사진을 찍으면 안 돼.
→ ② 흐름상 '그럴 필요가 없다'라는 뜻이 되어야 자연스럽다.
주어(We)가 복수이므로 do not(don't) have to가 적절하다.

chapter ❸ 수동태

❶ 수동태의 쓰임과 형태

1 1 cleans / is cleaned 2 use / are used
3 fixes / are fixed
2 1 is cooked 2 are visited 3 is elected
4 are washed

❷ 수동태의 시제

1 1 am invited / was invited / will be invited
2 are made / were made / will be made
2 1 will be sent 2 are, repaired
3 were bought 4 was stolen
5 will be planted

영작 기본 훈련

STEP 1

1 ⓐ hold   ⓑ is held
2 ⓐ wrote   ⓑ were written by
3 ⓐ will catch   ⓑ will be caught by
4 ⓐ sell   ⓑ are sold by us
5 ⓐ will design   ⓑ will be designed by
6 ⓐ bit   ⓑ was bitten by
7 ⓐ make   ⓑ are made by
8 ⓐ broke   ⓑ was broken by her

STEP 2

1 was drawn by a famous cartoonist
2 Strawberry cakes are baked by Mr. Green
3 The bird was hit by a car
4 Beautiful roses are grown by my grandparents
5 The difficult problem will be solved by him.

STEP 3

1 Our schedule will be changed.
2 This wall was painted by volunteers.
3 Most oil is produced in the Middle East.
4 My cell phone was found under the pillow.
5 The project will be managed by Tony.

1   **1** was sent / was not sent / Was, sent

      2 are baked / are not baked / Are, baked

      3 was taken / was not taken / When was, taken

2   **1** can be solved   **2** may be delivered

      3 must(should) be protected

4 by 이외의 전치사를 쓰는 수동태   p. 41

1   **1** scared of   **2** known as   **3** satisfied with

      4 filled with

2   **1** are worried about   **2** will be crowded with

      3 was not surprised at(by)   **4** Are, interested in

영작 기본 훈련   pp. 42~43

STEP 1

1   ⓐ are allowed   ⓑ are not allowed

    ⓒ Are, allowed

2   ⓐ is interested in   ⓑ Is, interested in

    ⓒ may be interested in

3   ⓐ Was, built   ⓑ was not built

    ⓒ When was, built

4   ⓐ was crowded with   ⓑ Was, crowded with

    ⓒ was not crowded with

5   ⓐ is spoken   ⓑ Is, spoken   ⓒ is not spoken

6   ⓐ was written   ⓑ Was, written

    ⓒ must(should) be written

STEP 2

1   was not invited   **2**   were satisfied with

3   Is, watched by   **4**   is filled with

5   can be, guessed

STEP 3

1   Fresh flowers are not sold

2   Was America discovered by Columbus?

3   The jacket can be washed by hand.

4   I am pleased with your success.

5   The medicine must be kept in the refrigerator.

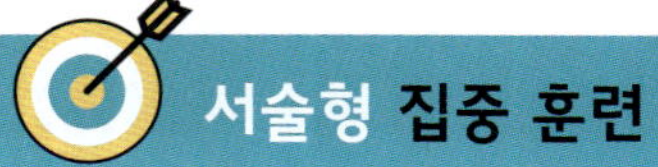

서술형 집중 훈련   pp. 44~45

집중 훈련 1

01 she → her   **02** by → about

03 held → be held

04 are allowed not → are not allowed

05 see → be seen   **06** Did → Were

07 by → in

집중 훈련 2

08 is filled with

09 was not(wasn't) designed by

10 is known as

11 Were the boxes moved

12 may be crowded with

13 were not(weren't) surprised at(by)

14 will be sold

집중 훈련 3

15 Her novel was not(wasn't) published last year.

16 The news should(must) be reported.

17 Colin is scared of bees.

18 Was the bike broken by him?

19 The sofa is covered with a white cloth.

20 Was the camera fixed?

21 Our school trip will be canceled.

집중 훈련 4

22 The song was sung by them.

23 Was he pleased with my gift?

24 The new movie will be released tomorrow.

25 She may be satisfied with her grade.

01 수동태의 행위자는 「by+목적격」으로 나타내므로 by her로 쓴다.

02 '~에 대해 걱정하다'는 be worried about으로 쓴다.

03 미래시제 수동태는 「will be+p.p.」로 쓴다.

04 수동태의 부정문은 「be동사+not+p.p.」로 쓴다.

05 바다가 '보이는' 것이므로 수동태로 써야 하며, 조동사가 있는 수동태는 「조동사+be+p.p.」로 쓴다.

06 후기가 '작성되는' 것이므로 수동태로 써야 하며, 수동태의 의문문은 「Be동사+주어+p.p. ~?」로 쓴다. 주어(the reviews)가

복수이고 과거시제이므로 be동사는 Were를 쓴다.

07 '~에 관심이 있다'는 be interested in으로 쓴다.

08 현재시제 수동태는 「am/are/is+p.p.」로 쓴다. '~로 가득 차다' 는 be filled with로 쓴다.

09 과거시제 수동태의 부정문은 「was /were+not+p.p.」로 쓴다. 수동태의 행위자 앞에는 by를 쓴다.

10 현재시제 수동태는 「am/are/is+p.p.」로 쓴다. '~로 알려지다' 는 be known as로 쓴다.

11 과거시제 수동태의 의문문은 「Was/Were+주어+p.p. ~?」로 쓴다.

12 조동사가 있는 수동태는 「조동사+be+p.p.」로 쓴다. '~로 붐비 다'는 be crowded with로 쓴다.

13 과거시제 수동태의 부정문은 「was/were+not+p.p.」로 쓴다. '~에 놀라다'는 be surprised at〔by〕로 쓴다.

14 미래시제 수동태는 「will be+p.p.」로 쓴다.

15 과거시제 수동태의 부정문은 「was/were+not+p.p.」로 쓴다.

16 소식이 '보도되는' 것이므로 수동태로 써야 하며, 조동사가 있는 수동태는 「조동사+be+p.p.」로 쓴다.

17 '~을 무서워하다'는 be scared of로 쓴다.

18 과거시제 수동태의 의문문은 「Was/Were+주어+p.p. ~?」로 쓴다. 수동태의 행위자는 「by+목적격」으로 쓴다.

19 '~로 덮여 있다'는 be covered with로 쓴다.

20 카메라가 '수리되는' 것이므로 수동태로 써야 하며, 과거시제 수 동태의 의문문은 「Was/Were+주어+p.p. ~?」로 쓴다.

21 미래시제 수동태는 「will be+p.p.」로 쓴다.

22 노래가 '불리는' 것이므로 수동태로 써야 하며, 수동태의 행위자 는 「by+목적격」으로 쓴다.

23 과거시제 수동태의 의문문은 「Was/Were+주어+p.p. ~?」로 쓴다. '~에 기뻐하다'는 be pleased with로 쓴다.

24 미래시제 수동태는 「will be+p.p.」로 쓴다.

25 조동사가 있는 수동태는 「조동사+be+p.p.」로 쓴다. '~에 만족 하다'는 be satisfied with로 쓴다.

1 English is spoken in many countries.

2 (1) Is, grown (2) are not〔aren't〕used
   (3) was called by

3 (1) My grandfather planted this tree.
   (2) This tree was planted by my grandfather.

4 Reservations can be made online.

5 were destroyed (by someone) 2,000 years ago

6 ② was painted → painted

1 영어가 '말해지는' 것이므로 「be동사+p.p.」형태의 수동태로 쓴다. 주어(English)가 3인칭 단수이고 현재시제이므로 be동사 는 is를 쓴다.

2 (1) 수동태의 의문문은 「Be동사+주어+p.p. ~?」로 쓴다.
   (2) 수동태의 부정문은 「be동사+not+p.p.」로 쓴다.
   (3) 과거시제 수동태는 「was/were+p.p.」로 쓰고, 수동태의 행위자 앞에는 by를 쓴다.

3 행위의 주체인 my grandfather가 주어인 능동태 문장과 행위 의 대상인 this tree가 주어인 수동태 문장을 각각 쓴다.

4 예약이 '이루어지는' 것이므로 수동태로 써야 하며, '~할 수 있다' 는 의미의 조동사 can을 사용하여 can be made로 쓴다.

5 과거시제 수동태는 「was/were+p.p.」로 쓰고, 행위자가 불분 명할 때는 「by+행위자」를 생략할 수 있다.

6 해석 '별이 빛나는 밤에'는 매우 유명한 그림이다. 그것은 Vincent van Gogh에 의해 그려졌다. 그는 그의 방 창문에서 그것을 그렸다. 그 그림은 1889년에 그려졌지만, 오늘날에도 많은 사람들에 의해 여전히 사랑받는다. 그 그림은 지금은 뉴욕 시의 한 박물관에 전시된다.
   → ② 주어(He)가 그림을 그린 것이므로 능동태 문장으로 써야 한다.

chapter **4** 문장의 구조

1 수여동사가 있는 문장   pp. 48~49

1 1 her, letters   2 me, my phone
    3 us, math   4 Jack, new shoes
    5 my family, dinner
2 1 gloves for him   2 me your passport
    3 us interesting stories   4 her many questions
    5 new backpacks for them
3 1 got some tea for her grandfather
    2 gave a nice hat to me
    3 passed me the water bottle
    4 lend you my textbook
    5 bring a blanket to me

영작 기본 훈련   pp.50~51

STEP 1

1 cooked us bulgogi / cooked bulgogi for
2 teaches them science / teaches science to
3 bought him a watch / bought a watch for
4 asked her a favor / asked a favor of
5 made us orange juice / made orange juice for

STEP 2

1 lent, his notebook
2 get some water for
3 pass me the salt
4 showed, to her classmates

STEP 3

1 cooked spaghetti for his girlfriend
2 He taught us some Chinese words.
3 My new neighbor asked a favor of me.
4 I bought T-shirts for my parents.
5 The clerk brought her a blue jacket.

2 목적격 보어가 있는 문장 1 | 명사·형용사   p. 52

1 1 my brother, Picasso   2 me, happy
    3 us, cool   4 our dog, Bear
2 1 made, angry(upset)   2 keep, clean
    3 found, sad

3 목적격 보어가 있는 문장 2 | to부정사   p. 53

1 1 그가 피아노 연주자가 되기를
    2 그녀에게 불을 꺼 달라고
    3 내가 그녀의 전화기를 사용하는 것을
    4 그들에게 그의 방에서 나가라고
    5 우리에게 날씨를 확인하라고
2 1 us to study   2 his players to take
    3 my mother to drive   4 him to go out
    5 them to stop

영작 기본 훈련   pp. 54~55

STEP 1

1 her an angel   2 him friendly
3 the window open   4 the book a bestseller
5 us to stand up   6 me to take
7 them to be quiet   8 me to get

STEP 2

1 keep us healthy   2 call me Casper
3 told him to lose   4 wanted them to move
5 allowed me to go

STEP 3

1 will keep the ice cream cold
2 He asked me to return his book.
3 We can make the world a better place.
4 She advised Tim to do his best.
5 I didn't expect you to come here.

1 **1** him dance(dancing)   **2** wind blow(blowing)
   3 them fight(fighting)   **4** us talk(talking)
2 **1** smelled, burning   **2** saw(watched), stop
   3 felt, licking   **4** heard, walk

5 **목적격 보어가 있는 문장 4 | 사역동사** p. 57

1 **1** us study   **2** her enter   **3** me sleep
   4 them work(to work)
2 **1** had, sit down   **2** let, use her laptop
   3 helps, grow(to grow)   **4** made, wait outside

영작 기본 훈련   pp. 58~59

STEP 1

1   saw(watched) her play(playing)
2   heard the bell ring(ringing)
3   felt raindrops fall(falling)
4   smelled something burning
5   let us play
6   made(had) them move
7   helped Kate find
8   made(had) him fix

STEP 2

1   had us walk our dog
2   felt something move(moving)
3   let her cat enter
4   saw Helen walk(walking)
5   made me do

STEP 3

1   let him choose the movie
2   made her wake up early
3   We saw the stars shining in the sky.
4   I heard someone following me.
5   He helped us to solve the problem.

집중 훈련 1

01 to me → me (또는 to me a skateboard →
   a skateboard to me)
02 write → to write
03 to → for (또는 delicious cookies to my friends →
   my friends delicious cookies)
04 freshly → fresh
05 turned → turn
06 setting → set(to set)
07 laughed → laugh(laughing)

집중 훈련 2

08 wanted them to join
09 bought chocolate for
10 made us happy   **11** showed me the way
12 call her a princess   **13** let his brother play
14 asked me to turn down

집중 훈련 3

15 Amy named her painting *Happiness*.
16 Tony felt his heart beat(beating) fast.
17 My sister had me charge her phone.
18 They keep the forest clean.
19 His dad allowed him to go camping.
20 I will send it to her tomorrow.
21 I saw him dance(dancing) in the park.

집중 훈련 4

22 Ted showed a magic trick to his friends.
23 She found the movie exciting.
24 We expect him to win the award.
25 Sarah heard a man shout(shouting) outside.

01 수여동사 give는 「give+간접목적어+직접목적어」 또는
「give+직접목적어+전치사(to)+간접목적어」 형태로 쓴다.
02 tell은 목적격 보어로 to부정사를 쓴다.
03 수여동사 make는 「make+간접목적어+직접목적어」 또는
「make+직접목적어+전치사(for)+간접목적어」 형태로 쓴다.
04 keep은 목적격 보어로 형용사를 쓴다. 목적격 보어가 '~하게'라
고 해석된다고 해서 부사를 쓰지 않도록 주의한다.

05 사역동사 have는 목적격 보어로 동사원형을 쓴다.

06 help는 목적격 보어로 동사원형과 to부정사 둘 다 쓸 수 있다.

07 지각동사 hear는 목적격 보어로 동사원형이나 현재분사를 쓴다.

08 want는 목적격 보어로 to부정사를 쓴다.

09 간접목적어(Eric)가 문장의 뒤에 있으므로 「buy+직접목적어+전치사(for)+간접목적어」 형태로 쓴다.

10 make는 「make+목적어+목적격 보어(형용사)」 형태로 쓴다.

11 직접목적어(the way to City Hall)의 일부가 문장의 뒤에 있으므로 「show+간접목적어+직접목적어」 형태로 쓴다.

12 call은 「call+목적어+목적격 보어(명사)」 형태로 쓴다. 목적격 보어가 명사일 때 목적어와 위치를 바꿔 쓰지 않도록 주의한다.

13 사역동사 let은 목적격 보어로 동사원형을 쓴다. let은 현재형과 과거형의 형태가 같은 동사이다.

14 ask는 목적격 보어로 to부정사를 쓴다.

15 name은 「name+목적어+목적격 보어(명사)」 형태로 쓴다.

16 지각동사 feel은 목적격 보어로 동사원형이나 현재분사를 쓴다.

17 사역동사 have는 목적격 보어로 동사원형을 쓴다.

18 keep은 「keep+목적어+목적격 보어(형용사)」 형태로 쓴다.

19 allow는 목적격 보어로 to부정사를 쓴다.

20 직접목적어가 대명사(it)일 때는 「주어+수여동사+직접목적어+전치사+간접목적어」의 형태로만 쓴다. send는 간접목적어 앞에 전치사 to를 쓰는 수여동사이다.

21 지각동사 see는 목적격 보어로 동사원형이나 현재분사를 쓴다.

22 전치사를 포함하라는 조건에 맞게 「show+직접목적어+전치사(to)+간접목적어」 형태로 쓴다.

23 find는 「find+목적어+목적격 보어(형용사)」 형태로 쓴다.

24 expect는 목적격 보어로 to부정사를 쓴다.

25 지각동사 hear는 목적격 보어로 동사원형이나 현재분사를 쓴다.

1 to bring → bring

2 saw a cat jump(jumping)

3 (1) ⓑ → sing(singing) a song

　　(2) ⓒ → made me sad

4 John allowed me to ride his bike.

5 let him(Joe) go

6 (1) My mom cooked my favorite food for me.

　　(2) My dad bought a smartphone for me.

　　(3) My sister gave a pair of headphones to me.

1 사역동사 have는 목적격 보어로 동사원형을 쓴다.

2 지각동사 see는 목적격 보어로 동사원형이나 현재분사를 쓴다.

3 (1) 지각동사 hear는 목적격 보어로 동사원형이나 현재분사를 쓴다.

　　(2) '~을 …하게 만들다'라는 의미의 문장은 「make+목적어+목적격 보어(형용사)」 형태로 쓴다.

4 allow는 목적격 보어로 to부정사를 쓴다.

5 해석 Joe 엄마, 이번 주말에 친구들과 영화 보러 가도 돼요?

엄마 물론이지.

→ 사역동사 let은 목적격 보어로 동사원형을 쓴다.

6 해석 Lisa 주말 잘 보냈니?

Ann 정말 잘 보냈어! 나의 엄마는 내가 가장 좋아하는 음식을 나에게 요리해 주셨어. 나의 아빠는 나에게 스마트폰을 사 주셨어. 나의 언니는 나에게 헤드폰 한 쌍을 주었고.

Lisa 와. 네 생일이었던 거야?

Ann 응, 그랬어.

→ 「주어+수여동사+직접목적어+전치사+간접목적어」 형태로 쓰며 cook과 buy는 간접목적어 앞에 전치사 for를, give는 전치사 to를 쓴다.

chapter ❺ to부정사

① to부정사의 명사적 용법 1　　　p. 64

1 **1** To ride roller coasters　**2** to read novels

　　3 to be a cook

2 **1** when to start　**2** what to buy　**3** how to make

② to부정사의 명사적 용법 2　　　p. 65

1 **1** It, to send　**2** It, to respect　**3** It, to stay

2 **1** of them to trust　**2** for us to get

　　3 of her to talk

영작 기본 훈련　　　pp. 66~67

STEP 1

A

1 ⓑ to plant many flowers　ⓒ to plant many flowers

2 ⓑ To learn Korean　ⓒ to learn Korean

3 ⓑ to draw cartoons　ⓒ to draw cartoons

B

1 ⓐ To　　ⓑ It, to write books　　ⓒ for her to write

2 ⓐ To　　ⓑ It, to say please　　ⓒ of you to say

3 ⓐ To　　ⓑ It, to donate money

　　ⓒ of them to donate

STEP 2

1 It, to skip　　　　**2** not to join

3 of her to teach　　**4** how to spend

5 to travel

STEP 3

1 They will decide where to meet.

2 I hope to run a marathon.

3 It is important for students to ask questions.

4 Sean's goal is to pass the test.

5 It was foolish of her to ignore the doctor's advice.

3 to부정사의 형용사적 용법　　p. 68

1 **1** somebody to meet　**2** a movie to watch

　　3 homework to finish　**4** a place to visit

2 **1** a topic to talk about　**2** a pen to write with

　　3 a chair to sit on　**4** someone to study with

4 to부정사의 부사적 용법　　p. 69

1 **1** 그 소식을 듣게 되어　**2** 실수를 하다니

　　3 너를 만나기 위해　**4** 조종사가 되었다

2 **1** to speak　**2** to spend　**3** to be

　　4 in order to repair

영작 기본 훈련　　pp. 70~71

STEP 1

A

1 to give　　　　**2** to buy

3 to write on　　**4** to listen to

B

1 to study　　　**2** to hear

3 to meet her

4 to become (be) a singer

STEP 2

1 activities to enjoy　　**2** silly to believe

3 to get there　　　　**4** friends to play with

5 surprised to win

STEP 3

1 I have nothing to do

2 We bought a house to live in.

3 The girl grew up to be a great scientist.

4 I was disappointed to see my low test score.

5 He went to the museum to see the paintings.

5 too ~ to부정사 구문　　p. 72

1 **1** too lazy / too lazy to work

　　2 too busy / too busy to cook

2 **1** too full to eat　**2** too young to drive

　　3 too sleepy to enjoy　**4** too heavy to lift

6 enough to부정사 구문　　p. 73

1 **1** kind enough / kind enough to help

　　2 hard enough / hard enough to build

2 **1** rich enough to buy

　　2 quietly enough to catch

　　3 wise enough to make

영작 기본 훈련　　pp. 74~75

STEP 1

1 ⓐ too weak to become

　　ⓑ strong enough to become

2 ⓐ too cold to eat　　ⓑ warm enough to eat

3 ⓐ too late to catch　　ⓑ early enough to catch

4 ⓐ too heavy to carry　　ⓑ light enough to carry

5 ⓐ too shy to sing　　ⓑ brave enough to sing

STEP 2

1 smart enough to solve

2 too slowly to finish

3 so good, she can go

4 too tired to clean

5 so busy, she couldn't eat

STEP 3

1 was too hungry to fall asleep
2 swam well enough to save my life
3 She is tall enough to be a volleyball player.
4 My brother is too young to watch this movie.
5 The box is big enough to hold all the books.

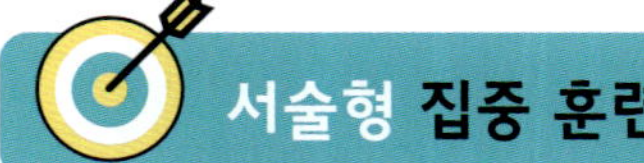
서술형 **집중 훈련**   pp. 76~77

집중 훈련 1

01 for → of
02 so → too
03 are → is
04 write → write with
05 visit → to visit
06 That → It
07 in order make → in order to make

집중 훈련 2

08 decided to go
09 too late to see
10 for him to swim
11 grew up to become
12 is to live
13 foolish to believe
14 a report to finish

집중 훈련 3

15 Let's talk about when to meet.
16 He is too short to ride the roller coaster.
17 We promised not (never) to fight again.
18 She is strong enough to move the bookshelf.
19 It is generous of her to give me a chance.
20 Can I use your phone to call Jane?
21 I have something to tell her.

집중 훈련 4

22 It is easy for him to learn new things.
23 I was too nervous to introduce myself.
24 They were sad to lose the game.
25 She didn't know where to put her bag.

01 사람의 성격 · 성향을 나타내는 형용사 뒤에는 to부정사의 의미상 주어로 「of+목적격」을 쓴다.

02 '너무 ~해서 …할 수 없는'은 「too+형용사+to부정사」로 나타내므로, so가 아닌 too가 되어야 한다.

03 주어로 쓰인 to부정사(구)는 항상 단수 취급하므로 is를 쓴다.

04 a pencil을 뒤에서 수식하는 형용사적 용법의 to부정사를 쓴다. write with a pencil의 의미이므로 to write 뒤에 전치사 with를 써야 한다.

05 형용사 excited 뒤에 감정의 원인을 나타내는 부사적 용법의 to부정사를 쓴다.

06 주어 역할을 하는 to부정사구를 뒤로 보내고 그 자리에는 가주어 It을 쓴다.

07 '~하기 위해'라는 목적의 의미를 강조할 때는 「in order to+동사원형」을 쓴다.

08 동사 decide의 목적어로 to부정사를 쓴다.

09 '…하기에 너무 ~하게'는 「too+부사+to부정사」로 쓴다.

10 to부정사의 의미상 주어는 일반적으로 「for+목적격」 형태로 to부정사 앞에 쓴다.

11 '(…해서) ~하다'라는 결과의 의미를 나타내는 부사적 용법의 to부정사를 쓴다.

12 be동사 뒤에 보어 역할을 하는 명사적 용법의 to부정사를 쓴다.

13 형용사 foolish 뒤에 '~하다니, ~하는 것을 보니'라는 판단의 근거를 나타내는 부사적 용법의 to부정사를 쓴다.

14 a report를 뒤에서 수식하는 형용사적 용법의 to부정사를 쓴다.

15 '언제 ~할지'는 「의문사+to부정사」를 써서 「when+to부정사」로 쓴다.

16 '…하기에 너무 ~한'은 「too+형용사+to부정사」로 나타낸다.

17 동사 promise의 목적어로 to부정사를 쓰고, to부정사 앞에 not (never)을 써서 부정의 의미를 나타낸다.

18 '…할 만큼 충분히 ~한'은 「형용사+enough+to부정사」로 쓴다.

19 가주어 it을 문장의 맨 앞에 쓰고 진주어인 to부정사구를 뒤에 쓴다. 사람의 성격 · 성향을 나타내는 형용사 뒤에는 to부정사의 의미상 주어로 「of+목적격」을 쓴다.

20 '~하기 위해'라는 목적을 나타내는 부사적 용법의 to부정사를 쓴다. 상대방의 허가를 구하는 표현은 Can I ~?로 쓴다.

21 something을 뒤에서 수식하는 형용사적 용법의 to부정사를 쓴다.

22 가주어 it을 문장의 맨 앞에 쓰고 진주어인 to부정사구를 뒤에 쓴다. to부정사의 의미상 주어는 「for+목적격」 형태로 to부정사 앞에 쓴다.

23 '너무 ~해서 …할 수 없는'은 「too+형용사+to부정사」로 쓴다.

24 형용사 sad 뒤에 감정의 원인을 나타내는 부사적 용법의 to부정사를 쓴다.

25 '어디에 ~할지'는 「where+to부정사」로 쓴다. 단어 수 조건에 맞게 didn't로 쓴다.

1 pleased to see
2 kind of you to listen to
3 (1) She grew up to become(be) an excellent swimmer.
   (2) There was nobody to help me.
4 (1) small enough to hold
   (2) to buy something to drink
5 (1) I was excited to play outside.
   (2) The water was too cold to swim in.

1 형용사 pleased 뒤에 감정의 원인을 나타내는 부사적 용법의 to부정사를 쓴다.
2 사람의 성격·성향을 나타내는 형용사 뒤에는 to부정사의 의미상 주어로 「of+목적격」을 쓴다.
3 (1) '(…해서) ~하다'라는 결과의 의미를 나타내는 부사적 용법의 to부정사를 쓴다.
   (2) nobody를 뒤에서 수식하는 형용사적 용법의 to부정사를 쓴다.
4 (1) '…할 만큼 충분히 ~한'은 「형용사+enough+to부정사」로 쓴다.
   (2) '~하기 위해'라는 목적을 나타내는 부사적 용법의 to부정사와 something을 뒤에서 수식하는 형용사적 용법의 to부정사를 써서 나타낸다.
5 해석 봄이라서 날씨가 따뜻하다. 지난 일요일에 나는 밖에서 놀게 되어서 신이 났다. 나는 수영을 하기 위해 강으로 갔다. 하지만 (수영을) 할 수 없었다. 물은 수영하기에 너무 차가웠다. 나는 집으로 와야 했다.
   → (1) 형용사 excited 뒤에 감정의 원인을 나타내는 부사적 용법의 to부정사를 쓴다.
   (2) '…하기에 너무 ~한'은 「too+형용사+to부정사」로 쓴다.

chapter 6 동명사

1 동명사의 쓰임   p. 80

1 1 Reading comic books   2 eating spicy food
   3 playing tennis
2 1 being   2 listening   3 Not wasting
   4 Living   5 walking

2 동명사 관용 표현   p. 81

1 1 worth trying   2 to visiting
   3 help laughing   4 like singing
2 1 busy studying   2 about going
   3 difficulty choosing   4 to working

영작 기본 훈련   pp. 82~83

STEP 1

A
1 ⓐ exercising   ⓑ exercising
2 ⓐ speaking English   ⓑ Speaking English
3 ⓐ helping us   ⓑ helping us
4 ⓐ playing soccer   ⓑ Playing soccer

B
1 ⓐ like watching   ⓑ about watching
2 ⓐ go surfing   ⓑ busy surfing
3 ⓐ used to eating   ⓑ forward to eating
4 ⓐ spent, buying   ⓑ worth buying

STEP 2

1 about downloading   2 Riding a bike
3 looking forward to hearing
4 enjoy going skiing
5 couldn't help smiling

STEP 3

1 not good at learning new languages
2 Taking photos is a good hobby.
3 She spends a lot of money buying clothes.
4 We are afraid of losing the game.
5 This novel is worth reading again.

1 **1** to come **2** drinking **3** eating
4 to meet **5** running **6** reading
2 **1** to travel **2** preparing **3** to study
4 sitting **5** to go

4 동명사와 to부정사 모두 목적어로 쓰는 동사   p. 85

1 **1** visiting **2** writing **3** walking(to walk)
4 watching(to watch) **5** saying
2 **1** to lock **2** washing(to wash)
3 to carry **4** snowing(to snow)

영작 기본 훈련   pp. 86~87

STEP 1

A

1 ⓑ painting the wall   ⓒ to paint the wall
2 ⓑ to book our flights
    ⓒ booking our flights
3 ⓑ sharing their food ⓒ to share their food

B

1 ⓐ forgot taking   ⓑ forgot to take
2 ⓐ tried to solve   ⓑ tried solving
3 ⓐ remembered buying   ⓑ remembered to buy
4 ⓐ stopped watching   ⓑ stopped to watch

STEP 2

1 promised to keep   **2** avoided telling
3 remember to turn off   **4** stopped throwing
5 forgot to send

STEP 3

1 gave up looking for work
2 expects to win the game
3 hated to go out
4 Would you mind turning down the volume?
5 She plans to attend your graduation ceremony.

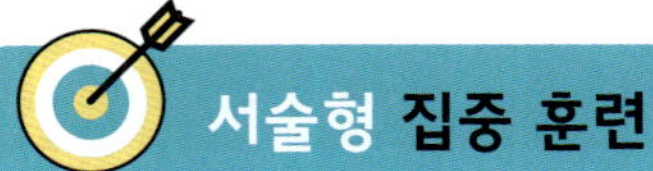

서술형 집중 훈련   pp. 88~89

집중 훈련 1

01 join → joining   **02** moving → to move
03 to eat → eating   **04** to put → putting
05 doing not → not doing
06 to camping → camping
07 to walk → walking

집중 훈련 2

08 I do not(don't) mind eating
09 looking forward to running
10 is worth sharing
11 They expect to discuss
12 I am(I'm) used to reading
13 I tried to understand
14 We could not(couldn't) help crying

집중 훈련 3

15 Dave does not(doesn't) enjoy talking on the phone.
16 We are busy planning our vacation.
17 She is afraid of taking elevators.
18 I am(I'm) interested in solving mysteries.
19 He keeps talking to himself.
20 How about going to the movies with me?
21 I remember meeting him at the party.

집중 훈련 4

22 Going to school festivals is exciting.
23 He wanted to avoid fighting with his friends.
24 She forgot to close the window last night. / Last night, she forgot to close the window.
25 We spent two hours cooking Mexican food.

01 전치사 about의 목적어로 동명사 joining을 쓴다.
02 동사 plan은 동명사가 아닌 to부정사를 목적어로 쓴다.
03 '~하고 싶다'는 「feel like -ing」로 쓴다.
04 '(과거에) ~한 것을 기억하다'라는 의미를 나타낼 때는 remember의 목적어로 동명사를 쓴다.
05 동명사 앞에 not을 써서 부정의 의미를 나타낸다.
06 '~하러 가다'는 「go -ing」로 쓴다.

07 동사 stop의 목적어로 동명사를 써서 '~하는 것을 멈추다'라는 의미를 나타낸다.

08 동사 mind의 목적어로 동명사를 쓴다.

09 '~하는 것을 고대하다'는 「look forward to -ing」로 쓴다. '~하고 있다'라는 의미는 현재진행형으로 나타낸다.

10 '~할 가치가 있다'는 「be worth -ing」로 쓴다.

11 동사 expect의 목적어로 to부정사를 쓴다.

12 '~하는 데 익숙하다'는 「be used to -ing」로 쓴다.

13 '~하려고 애쓰다'라는 의미를 나타낼 때는 try의 목적어로 to부정사를 쓴다.

14 '~하지 않을 수 없다'는 「cannot〔can't〕 help -ing」로 쓴다. 과거시제이므로 could not〔couldn't〕를 쓴다.

15 동사 enjoy의 목적어로 동명사를 쓴다.

16 '~하느라 바쁘다'는 「be busy -ing」로 쓴다.

17 전치사 of의 목적어로 동명사를 쓴다.

18 전치사 in의 목적어로 동명사를 쓴다.

19 동사 keep의 목적어로 동명사를 쓴다. (talk to oneself: 혼잣말을 하다)

20 '~하는 게 어때?'는 「How〔What〕 about -ing?」로 쓴다.

21 '(과거에) ~한 것을 기억하다'라는 의미를 나타낼 때는 remember의 목적어로 동명사를 쓴다.

22 동명사를 써서 주어를 나타낸다. 주어로 쓰인 동명사(구)는 항상 단수 취급하므로 be동사는 is를 쓴다.

23 want의 목적어로 to부정사(to avoid)를 쓰고, avoid의 목적어로 동명사(fighting)를 쓴다.

24 '(미래에) ~할 것을 잊다'라는 의미를 나타낼 때는 forget의 목적어로 to부정사를 쓴다.

25 '~하는 데 시간을 쓰다'는 「spend+시간+-ing」로 나타낸다.

1 good at remembering words

2 are → is

3 (1) I have difficulty falling asleep.
(2) She is not used to getting up early.

4 couldn't, eating

5 (1) (a) going (b) practicing (c) to win
(d) preparing (e) saying
(2) I will look forward to hearing good news.

1 전치사 at의 목적어로 동명사 remembering을 쓴다. (~을 잘하다: be good at)

2 주어로 쓰인 동명사(구)는 항상 단수 취급하므로 be동사는 is를 쓴다.

3 (1) ~하는 데 어려움을 겪다: have difficulty -ing
(2) ~하는 데 익숙하다: be used to -ing

4 '~하지 않을 수 없다'는 「cannot〔can't〕 help -ing」로 쓴다. 과거시제이므로 couldn't를 쓴다.

5 **해석** Alice Tony, 스케이트보드 타러 가는 게 어때?
Tony 미안하지만, 나는 갈 수 없어. 난 피곤해. 하루 종일 피아노 연습하느라 바빴거든.
Alice 그거 안됐구나.
Tony 다음 주 수요일에 대회가 있어. 거기서 우승하기를 바라고 있어.
Alice 그럼 대회를 위해 계속 연습하는 게 좋겠다.
Tony 맞아. 다음 주말에 스케이트보드 타러 가자!
Alice 좋아. 나는 좋은 소식을 듣기를 고대할게.
Tony 그렇게 말해줘서 고마워.
→ (1) (a) '~하는 게 어때?'는 「How about -ing?」로 쓴다.
(b) '~하느라 바쁘다'는 「be busy -ing」로 쓴다.
(c) 동사 hope의 목적어로 to부정사를 쓴다.
(d) 동사 keep의 목적어로 동명사를 쓴다.
(e) 전치사 for의 목적어로 동명사를 쓴다.
(2) '~하기를 고대하다'는 「look forward to -ing」로 쓴다.

1 분사의 형태와 종류 p. 92

1 **1** falling / fallen **2** cooking / cooked
3 painting / painted **4** growing / grown
2 **1** barking **2** broken **3** flying **4** used

2 분사의 쓰임 p. 93

1 **1** made **2** playing **3** burned(burnt)
4 laughing **5** buried **6** lost **7** closed

영작 기본 훈련 pp. 94~95

STEP 1

1 swimming **2** made
3 sitting **4** lost
5 talking **6** called
7 running **8** growing

STEP 2

1 boiling water **2** castle built
3 clouds covering **4** rising star
5 broken vase

STEP 3

1 take the money left on the table
2 is a picture hanging on the wall
3 Many trained animals appear in this movie.
4 The singer smiled at the shouting fans.
5 The diamonds sold at the store were fake.

3 감정을 나타내는 분사 pp. 96~97

1 **1** interested / interesting **2** touching / touched
3 disappointed / disappointing
2 **1** boring **2** satisfying **3** shocked
4 amazing **5** excited
3 **1** satisfied with **2** interesting books
3 disappointed with **4** surprising news
5 amazed look

영작 기본 훈련 pp. 98~99

STEP 1

1 ⓐ shocked ⓑ shocking
2 ⓐ interesting ⓑ interested
3 ⓐ disappointed ⓑ disappointing
4 ⓐ surprising ⓑ surprised
5 ⓐ exciting ⓑ excited
6 ⓐ bored ⓑ boring
7 ⓐ amazing ⓑ amazed
8 ⓐ satisfied ⓑ satisfying

STEP 2

1 excited to go for a walk
2 We were bored with the same food
3 The ending of the movie wasn't satisfying.
4 The project ended with disappointing results.
5 Meeting the scientist in person was amazing.

STEP 3

1 I was surprised by
2 They are interested in
3 a shocking story
4 study boring subjects
5 were amazed by Mount Everest

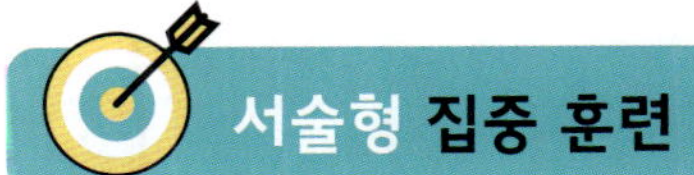

서술형 집중 훈련

집중 훈련 1

01 hiding → hidden **02** surprised → surprising

03 fell → fallen **04** printing → printed

05 shocking → shocked

06 stealing → stolen **07** naming → named

집중 훈련 2

08 look amazing **09** a lot of used items

10 shouting for help **11** the sleeping baby

12 filled with people

13 her failure was disappointing

14 The injured player

집중 훈련 3

15 The book is full of exciting stories.

16 She is interested in personality tests.

17 The boy playing computer games is Brian.

18 This is a novel written in English.

19 The students were satisfied with the school festival.

20 Did you see the broken window?

21 The characters were boring.

집중 훈련 4

22 Who is that boy dancing with Vicky?

23 They were surprised by the shocking news.

24 I bought a watch made in Germany.

25 The excited fans ran onto the field.

01 '숨겨진'이라는 수동의 의미이므로 과거분사 hidden을 쓴다.

02 주어가 감정을 유발하는 것이므로 현재분사 surprising을 쓴다.

03 '떨어진'이라는 완료의 의미이므로 과거분사 fallen을 쓴다.

04 '인쇄된'이라는 수동 및 완료의 의미이므로 과거분사 printed를 쓴다.

05 주어가 감정을 느끼는 것이므로 과거분사 shocked를 쓴다.

06 '도난당한'이라는 수동 및 완료의 의미이므로 과거분사 stolen을 쓴다.

07 '이름 붙여진'이라는 수동의 의미이므로 과거분사 named를 쓴다.

08 주어가 감정을 유발하는 것이므로 현재분사 amazing을 쓴다.

09 '중고의, 사용된'이라는 수동 및 완료의 의미이므로 과거분사 used를 쓴다.

10 '외치는'이라는 능동 및 진행의 의미이므로 현재분사 shouting을 쓴다.

11 '자고 있는'이라는 능동 및 진행의 의미이므로 현재분사 sleeping을 명사 baby 앞에 쓴다.

12 '가득 채워진'이라는 수동 및 완료의 의미이므로 과거분사 filled를 쓴다.

13 주어가 감정을 유발하는 것이므로 현재분사 disappointing을 쓴다.

14 '다친, 부상당한'이라는 수동 및 완료의 의미이므로 과거분사 injured를 명사 player 앞에 쓴다.

15 수식받는 명사(stories)가 감정을 유발하는 것이므로 현재분사 exciting을 명사 앞에 쓴다.

16 주어가 감정을 느끼는 것이므로 과거분사 interested를 쓴다.

17 '컴퓨터 게임을 하고 있는'이라는 능동 및 진행의 의미이므로 명사(The boy)를 뒤에서 수식하는 현재분사구 playing computer games를 쓴다.

18 '영어로 쓰인'이라는 수동 및 완료의 의미이므로 명사(a novel)를 뒤에서 수식하는 과거분사구 written in English를 쓴다.

19 주어가 감정을 느끼는 것이므로 과거분사 satisfied를 쓴다.

20 '깨진'이라는 수동 및 완료의 의미이므로 과거분사 broken을 명사 window 앞에 쓴다.

21 주어가 감정을 유발하는 것이므로 현재분사 boring을 쓴다.

22 '춤추고 있는'이라는 능동 및 진행의 의미이므로 명사(that boy)를 뒤에서 수식하는 현재분사구 dancing with Vicky를 쓴다.

23 주어가 감정을 느끼는 것이므로 과거분사 surprised를 be동사 뒤에 쓰고, 수식받는 명사(news)가 감정을 유발하는 것이므로 현재분사 shocking을 명사 앞에 쓴다.

24 '만들어진'이라는 수동 및 완료의 의미이므로 명사(a watch)를 뒤에서 수식하는 과거분사구 made in Germany를 쓴다.

25 수식받는 명사(fans)가 감정을 느끼는 것이므로 과거분사 excited를 명사 fans 앞에 쓴다.

1 (1) called (2) sitting
2 shocked → shocking
3 written, interesting
4 (1) painting (2) painted
5 The singer's new song is disappointing.
6 (1) exciting, satisfied
　　(2) surprised, pleased

1 (1) '불리는'이라는 수동의 의미이므로 과거분사 called를 쓴다.
　　(2) '앉아 있는'이라는 능동 및 진행의 의미이므로 현재분사 sitting을 쓴다.
2 주어가 감정을 유발하는 것이므로 현재분사 shocking을 쓴다.
3 '~에 의해 쓰인'이라는 수동의 의미이므로 명사(This novel)를 뒤에서 수식하는 과거분사 written을 쓰고, 주어가 감정을 유발하는 것이므로 be동사 뒤에 현재분사 interesting을 쓴다.
4 (1) '~하고 있다'라는 능동 및 진행의 의미이므로 현재분사로 쓴다.
　　(2) '~에 의해 그려진'이라는 수동 및 완료의 의미이므로 과거분사로 쓴다.
5 주어가 감정을 유발하는 것이므로 disappoint를 현재분사로 쓴다.
6 해석 오늘은 엄마의 생신이다. 우리 가족은 영화를 보러 갔다. 그 영화가 흥미진진해서 우리는 그것에 만족했다. 집에 돌아온 후, 우리는 엄마를 위해 파티를 열었고, 그녀에게 선물들을 드렸다. 그녀는 그 선물들에 놀랐고 파티에 기뻐했다.
→ (1) 영화가 감정을 유발하는 것이므로 현재분사 exciting을, 우리는 감정을 느끼는 것이므로 과거분사 satisfied를 쓴다.
(2) 주어가 감정을 느끼는 것이므로 둘 다 과거분사로 쓴다.

chapter **8** 비교

1 원급 비교   p. 104

1 **1** as thin as   **2** as cold as
　　3 not as(so) quiet as   **4** not as(so) strong as
2 **1** as safe as   **2** as high as possible
　　3 not as(so) busy as

2 배수 비교   p. 105

1 **1** as fast as / three times as fast as
　　2 as large as / twice as large as
　　3 as expensive as / four times as expensive as
2 **1** five times as thick as
　　2 three times as quickly as
　　3 twice as heavy as
　　4 three times as old as

영작 기본 훈련   pp. 106~107

STEP 1

1 as young as　　　　**2** not as(so) short as
3 as soon as possible
4 three times as big as
5 as fast as　　　　**6** twice as high as
7 as slowly as she could
8 not as(so) healthy as

STEP 2

1 as well as　　　　**2** as expensive as
3 as regularly as we can　**4** twice as long as
5 not as(so) difficult as

STEP 3

1 is not so shy as me
2 is thirty times as big as this model one
3 is four times as deep as the kids' pool
4 kicked the ball as far as he could
5 Brian gets up as early as possible.

1 1 cooler than   2 more famous than
    3 better than   4 more quietly than
2 1 more comfortable than   2 smaller and smaller
    3 The more, the happier

4 최상급 비교   p. 109

1 1 the funniest   2 the most diligent
    3 the worst   4 the most dangerous
    5 the nicest   6 the smartest
2 1 the most expensive   2 the largest
    3 the strongest   4 the most delicious

영작 기본 훈련   pp. 110~111

STEP 1

1 ⓑ shorter than   ⓒ the shortest
2 ⓑ busier than   ⓒ busier and busier
3 ⓑ more interesting than   ⓒ the most interesting
4 ⓑ hotter than   ⓒ one of the hottest
5 ⓑ more and more important
   ⓒ one of the most important
6 ⓑ much(even/still/far) harder than
   ⓒ The harder, the better

STEP 2

1 is one of the biggest cities in Korea
2 the better you will do
3 She drives more slowly than her sister.
4 The store will get more and more crowded.
5 His idea is far more creative than this one.

STEP 3

1 cried louder and louder
2 is more expensive than his old one
3 is much(even/still/far/a lot) taller than the kid
4 It is one of the most exciting games
5 The more you exercise, the healthier

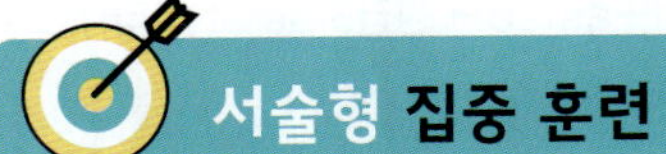

서술형 집중 훈련   pp. 112~113

집중 훈련 1

01 busiest → the busiest   02 better → well
03 most important → more important
04 so not → not so(as)   05 problem → problems
06 twice big → twice as big
07 very → much(even/still/far/a lot)

집중 훈련 2

08 later than Jim   09 as light as a feather
10 more and more interesting
11 as cool as a movie
12 the most popular festival
13 The longer, the more tired
14 one of the most famous actors

집중 훈련 3

15 Wash your hands as often as possible.
16 Her room is three times larger than mine.
17 Leon is the best player on his team.
18 His score is twice as high as mine.
19 The earlier you start, the earlier you will finish.
20 It is one of the most beautiful beaches in the world.
21 The Earth is much(even/still/far/a lot) bigger than the Moon.

집중 훈련 4

22 The weather is getting warmer and warmer.
23 This is the tallest building in this city.
24 This vase is four times as expensive as that dish.
25 I tried to speak as clearly as I could.

01 '가장 ~한'은 「the+최상급」으로 나타내므로 busiest 앞에 the 를 쓴다.
02 '…만큼 ~하게'는 「as+원급+as」로 나타내므로 원급인 well을 쓴다. 동사 cooks를 수식하고 있으므로 형용사 good이 아닌 부사 well을 써야 한다.
03 '…보다 더 ~한'은 「비교급+than」으로 나타내며, important의 비교급은 more important이다.

04 '…만큼 ~하지 않은'은 「not+as〔so〕+원급+as」로 나타내므로 not so〔as〕cold as로 쓴다.

05 '가장 ~한 … 중 하나'는 「one of the+최상급+복수명사」로 나타내므로 복수명사 problems로 쓴다.

06 '…보다 (몇) 배 더 ~한'는 「배수사+as+원급+as」로 나타내므로 twice와 big 사이에 as를 쓴다.

07 비교급을 강조할 때는 very가 아닌 much, even, still, far, a lot 등을 쓴다.

08 '…보다 더 ~하게'는 「비교급+than」으로 쓴다.

09 '…만큼 ~한'은 「as+원급+as」로 쓴다.

10 '점점 더 ~한'은 「비교급+and+비교급」으로 쓴다. 비교급의 형태가 「more+원급」인 경우에는 「more and more+원급」으로 쓴다.

11 '…만큼 ~한'은 「as+원급+as」로 쓴다.

12 '가장 ~한'은 「the+최상급」으로 쓴다. popular의 최상급은 most popular이다.

13 '~할수록 더 …하다'는 「the+비교급 ~, the+비교급 …」으로 쓴다. tired의 비교급은 more tired이다.

14 '가장 ~한 … 중 하나'는 「one of the+최상급+복수명사」로 쓴다. famous의 최상급은 most famous이다.

15 '가능한 한 ~하게'는 「as+원급+as possible」로 쓴다.

16 than을 이용한 '…보다 (몇) 배 더 ~한'은 「배수사+비교급+than」으로 쓴다. '세 배'는 three times로 쓴다.

17 '가장 ~한'은 「the+최상급」으로 쓴다. good의 최상급은 best이다.

18 as를 이용한 '…보다 (몇) 배 더 ~한'은 「배수사+as+원급+as」로 쓴다. '두 배'는 twice로 쓴다.

19 '~할수록 더 …하다'는 「the+비교급 ~, the+비교급 …」으로 쓴다

20 '가장 ~한 … 중 하나'는 「one of the+최상급+복수명사」로 쓴다.

21 '…보다 더 ~한'은 「비교급+than」으로 쓴다. 비교급을 강조할 때는 비교급 앞에 much, even, still, far, a lot 등을 쓴다.

22 '점점 더 ~한'은 「비교급+and+비교급」으로 쓴다.

23 '가장 ~한'은 「the+최상급」으로 쓴다.

24 as를 이용한 '…보다 (몇) 배 더 ~한'은 「배수사+as+원급+as」로 쓴다. '네 배'는 four times로 쓴다.

25 can을 이용한 '가능한 한 ~하게'는 「as+원급+as+주어+can」으로 나타낸다. 과거시제이므로 could를 쓴다.

1 shorter and shorter

2 He is one of the most talented students in my school.

3 (1) the smallest　(2) the cheapest　(3) the largest

4 (1) twice as long as hers　(2) as fast as possible

5 (1) the tallest tree in the garden
(2) It was not as〔so〕tall as me
(3) it is much〔even/still/far/a lot〕taller than me

---

1 점점 더 ~한: 비교급+and+비교급

2 가장 ~한 … 중 하나: one of the+최상급+복수명사

3 (1) 방 크기가 가장 작으므로 the smallest를 쓴다.
(2) 방 가격이 가장 저렴하므로 the cheapest를 쓴다.
(3) 방 크기가 가장 크므로 the largest를 쓴다

4 (1) …보다 (몇) 배 더 ~한: 배수사+as+원급+as
(2) 가능한 한 ~하게: as+원급+as possible

5 해석　나의 할머니의 정원에는 많은 나무들과 꽃들이 있다. 그 정원에 있는 한 나무는 나머지들보다 눈에 띈다. 그것은 정원에서 가장 키가 큰 나무이다. 할머니는 내가 어린 소녀였을 때 그 나무를 심으셨다. 그때 그것은 나만큼 키가 크지 않았다. 지금 그것은 나보다 더 훨씬 키가 크다. 화창한 날이면 우리는 그 나무 아래에 앉아 있는 것을 좋아한다.
→ (1) 가장 ~한: the+최상급
(2) …만큼 ~하지 않은: not+as〔so〕+원급+as
(3) …보다 훨씬 더 ~한: much〔even/still/far/a lot〕+비교급+than

chapter ❾ 접속사

① 등위접속사　　p. 116

1️⃣ 1 but　2 and　3 or　4 so
2️⃣ 1 nice but expensive　2 or make it
　　3 and ate ice cream　4 so everyone loves her

② 상관접속사　　p. 117

1️⃣ 1 어른들뿐만 아니라 어린이들도
　　2 영어가 아니라 프랑스어
　　3 맛있을 뿐만 아니라 건강에도 좋은
　　4 내 것도 네 것도 아닌
2️⃣ 1 either, or　2 neither, nor　3 Both, and
　　4 not, but

영작 기본 훈련　　pp. 118~119

STEP 1

1 so he couldn't take　2 delicious but too salty
3 or order pizza　4 both math and science
5 not angry but disappointed
6 neither Spain nor France
7 not only smart but also kind
8 either the subway or a taxi

STEP 2

1 I waited for her, but she didn't show up.
2 My brother likes both soccer and basketball.
3 Either you or Tony has to finish the report.
4 It is cold as well as rainy.
5 This camera is neither heavy nor expensive.

STEP 3

1 is good for both body and mind
2 is not fiction but fact
3 We can (either) eat out or go shopping
4 so I cannot(can't) check my email
5 bought not only some flowers but also a cake

③ 명사절을 이끄는 접속사 that　　p. 120

1️⃣ 1 that he won the race
　　2 (that) the room was empty
　　3 that we have enough time
2️⃣ 1 that she passed　2 knows that I called
　　3 His strength is that

④ 부사절을 이끄는 접속사　　p. 121

1️⃣ 1 when　2 if　3 because(as)　4 after
2️⃣ 1 while he was playing　2 unless you take
　　3 Before we visited

영작 기본 훈련　　pp. 122~123

STEP 1

A

1 (that) she is a fashion model
2 that his voice is too loud
3 that he died

B

1 before I go to bed
2 if you are bored　3 when I got home
4 because(as) she failed the test
5 while he was exercising

STEP 2

1 when you go out
2 Unless you eat breakfast
3 while I was sleeping
4 that everyone lives in peace
5 Because(As) it was cold

STEP 3

1 If you want to read this book
2 It is amazing that my brother got a job.
3 You have to warm up before you swim. / Before you swim, you have to warm up.
4 You will feel lonely if you have no friends. / If you have no friends, you will feel lonely.
5 The sad thing is that I can't understand him.

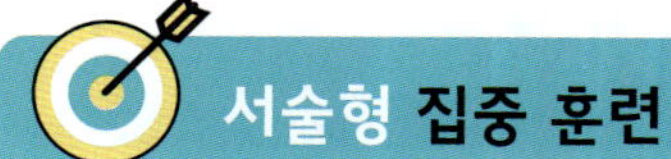

집중 훈련 1

01 so → because(as)   **02** or → nor
03 before → after   **04** will get → get
05 wants → want   **06** read → reading
07 don't walk → walk (또는 unless → if)

집중 훈련 2

08 when he visited me
09 but he does not(doesn't) like them
10 not only in Korea but also in Europe
11 before the guests arrive
12 because(as) I did not(didn't) give up
13 know (that) he likes chocolate
14 both sunlight and water

집중 훈련 3

15 When I was young, I lived in China. / I lived in China when I was young.
16 While she was taking a walk, she got lost. / She got lost while she was taking a walk.
17 The problem is that she is not(isn't) honest.
18 If she joins our team, I will be happy. / I will be happy if she joins our team.
19 Either she or I have to cook dinner.
20 Unless I am(I'm) busy, I will help you. / I will help you unless I am(I'm) busy.
21 She likes neither pizza nor fried chicken.

집중 훈련 4

22 We will either go swimming or play basketball.
23 She loves camping as well as hiking.
24 It was shocking that we lost the game.
25 This is not a movie but a play.

01 '~ 이기 때문에'를 의미하는 접속사 because(as)를 쓴다.
02 'A도 B도 아닌'은 「neither A nor B」로 나타내므로 nor를 쓴다.
03 '~한 후에'를 의미하는 접속사 after를 쓴다.
04 시간을 나타내는 부사절에서는 현재시제를 써서 미래의 일을 나타내므로 동사는 get을 쓴다.

05 「both A and B」가 주어로 쓰인 경우 복수 취급하므로 want를 쓴다.
06 등위접속사로 연결되는 부분은 문법적으로 대등한 형태여야 하므로 enjoy의 목적어인 동명사 watching과 마찬가지로 reading을 쓴다.
07 unless는 '만약 ~하지 않으면'이라는 부정의 의미이므로 동사에 부정어를 쓰지 않는다. unless는 if ~ not으로도 쓸 수 있다.
08 '~할 때'를 의미하는 접속사 when을 쓴다.
09 역접의 의미를 나타내는 등위접속사 but을 쓴다.
10 'A뿐만 아니라 B도'를 의미하는 「not only A but also B」를 쓴다.
11 '~하기 전에'를 의미하는 접속사 before를 쓴다. 시간을 나타내는 부사절에서는 현재시제를 써서 미래의 일을 나타내므로 동사는 arrive를 쓴다.
12 '~하기 때문에'를 의미하는 접속사 because(as)를 쓴다.
13 동사 know의 목적어로 접속사 that이 이끄는 명사절을 쓰며, 이때 that은 생략할 수 있다.
14 'A와 B 둘 다'를 의미하는 「both A and B」를 쓴다.
15 '~할 때'를 의미하는 접속사 when을 쓴다. 부사절이 주절 앞에 올 때는 부사절 끝에 콤마(,)를 쓴다.
16 '~하는 동안'을 의미하는 접속사 while을 쓴다.
17 문장의 보어로 be동사 뒤에 접속사 that이 이끄는 명사절을 쓴다.
18 '만약 ~하면'을 의미하는 접속사 if를 쓴다. 조건을 나타내는 부사절에서는 현재시제를 써서 미래의 일을 나타내므로 동사는 joins를 쓴다.
19 'A나 B 둘 중 하나'를 의미하는 「either A or B」가 주어로 쓰인 경우 동사는 B에 수 일치시키므로 have to를 쓴다.
20 unless는 '만약 ~하지 않으면'이라는 부정의 의미이므로 동사에 부정어를 쓰지 않는다. 조건을 나타내는 부사절에서는 현재시제를 써서 미래의 일을 나타내므로 동사는 am을 쓴다.
21 'A도 B도 아닌'을 의미하는 「neither A nor B」를 쓰고, 부정의 의미이므로 동사에 부정어를 쓰지 않는다.
22 선택의 의미를 나타내는 등위접속사 or를 사용하거나 'A나 B 둘 중 하나'를 의미하는 「either A or B」를 쓸 수 있다. 단어 수 조건에 맞게 either를 포함하여 쓴다.
23 as를 포함한 'A뿐만 아니라 B도'는 「B as well as A」로 나타낸다.
24 문장의 주어로 접속사 that이 이끄는 명사절을 쓴다. 가주어 it을 문장의 맨 앞에 쓰고, 진주어인 that절은 뒤로 보낸다.
25 'A가 아니라 B'를 의미하는 「not A but B」를 쓴다.

1 (1) When the doorbell rings

(2) because she played computer games

2 (1) after the rain stopped

(2) but he didn't reply

(3) while you're crossing the street

3 If you do your best, you will get a good grade.

4 I didn't know that the library is closed on
Sundays.

5 (1) as well as (2) Not, but

(3) Neither, nor (4) Both, and

1 (1) '~할 때'를 의미하는 접속사 when을 쓴다.

(2) '~하기 때문에'를 의미하는 접속사 because를 쓴다.

2 (1) ~한 후에: after (2) 그러나: but

(3) ~하는 동안: while

3 '만약 ~하면'이라는 의미의 조건을 나타내는 접속사 if를 쓴다. 부
사절이 주절 앞에 올 때는 부사절 끝에 콤마(,)를 쓴다. 조건을 나
타내는 부사절에서는 현재시제를 써서 미래의 일을 나타내므로
동사는 do를 쓴다.

4 동사 know의 목적어로 접속사 that이 이끄는 명사절을 써서
연결한다.

5 (1) A뿐만 아니라 B도: B as well as A

(2) A가 아니라 B: not A but B

(3) A도 B도 아닌: neither A nor B

(4) A와 B 둘 다: both A and B

chapter **10** 관계대명사

1 주격 관계대명사 who   p. 128

1 **1** 나무 뒤에 있던 아이   **2** 테니스를 치는 사람들

3 여행을 많이 다니는 여자   **4** 드레스를 입고 있는 소녀

2 **1** who(that) lives in Sydney

2 who(that) are swimming in the pool

3 who(that) is popular in China

2 목적격 관계대명사 whom   p. 129

1 **1** 내가 만나고 싶은 아이들   **2** 그가 결혼한 여자

3 내가 아는 사람들   **4** 그녀가 방문한 의사

2 **1** who(m)(that) I trust

2 who(m)(that) she met

3 who(m)(that) you like

4 who(m)(that) I respect

5 who(m)(that) the truck hit

영작 기본 훈련   pp. 130~131

STEP 1

1 who won   **2** who(m) I drew

3 who wrote   **4** who(m) they found

5 who stepped   **6** who(m) Sandy met

7 who is wearing

STEP 2

1 who(that) waited

2 who(m)(that) I called

3 who(that) can solve

4 who(m)(that) you helped

5 who(that) is waving

STEP 3

1 a man who looked like my uncle

2 The student whom I taught

3 the girl who is singing on the stage

4 a person that we invited

5 The woman who lives on the second floor

3 관계대명사 which

p. 132

1 **1** which(that) has　**2** which(that) sells
　　3 which(that) were　**4** which(that) looks
2 **1** which(that) I use
　　2 which(that) he is carrying
　　3 which(that) I learned

4 소유격 관계대명사 whose

p. 133

1 **1** 눈이 아름다운 소년　**2** 바퀴가 큰 자전거
　　3 문이 고장 난 자동차　**4** 제목이 너무 긴 영화
2 **1** whose members were　**2** whose screen is
　　3 whose hobby is　**4** whose workers are
　　5 whose legs are

영작 기본 훈련

pp. 134~135

STEP 1

1　which(that) sells candles
2　which(that) she baked
3　whose father works
4　which(that) he bought
5　which(that) has
6　my mom made
7　which(that) are popular

STEP 2

1　the key which(that) you lost
2　a laptop whose keyboard
3　which(that) dries quickly
4　whose storylines are simple
5　The food we ate

STEP 3

1　that Tony wrote was about space
2　has a cat whose ears are big
3　I have a friend whose sister is a police officer.
4　The building they visited has a long history.
5　The restaurant uses vegetables that are in season.

5 관계대명사 that

p. 136

1 **1** 내가 캠프에서 만난 바로 그 소년
　　2 내가 경험한 최고의 순간
　　3 그 질문에 답한 유일한 학생
2 **1** the biggest cake that　**2** the same watch that
　　3 nobody that　**4** all the money that
　　5 the only friend that

6 관계대명사 what

p. 137

1 **1** that(which) / what he made
　　2 that(which) / what I'm wearing
2 **1** What I want　**2** what you read
　　3 what I believe

영작 기본 훈련

pp. 138~139

STEP 1

1　ⓐ what he wrote　　ⓑ that he wrote
2　ⓐ that you drew　　ⓑ What you drew
3　ⓐ what they built　　ⓑ that they built
4　ⓐ What he cooked　　ⓑ that he cooked
5　ⓐ that I wanted　　ⓑ what I wanted
6　ⓐ that he said　　ⓑ what he said
7　ⓐ What you did　　ⓑ that you did
8　ⓐ what he made　　ⓑ that he made

STEP 2

1　what I expected
2　anything that we can do
3　tell me what you need
4　the only movie that made
5　What they sell is

STEP 3

1　The child opened all the presents that he got
2　was different from what people believed
3　the very house that Dan was born in
4　The teacher checked what we wrote.
5　Look at the girl and the dog that are running.

집중 훈련 1

01 which → who(that)
02 who → that(which) 또는 who 삭제
03 who → whose   **04** That → What
05 likes → like
06 which → who(m)(that) 또는 which 삭제
07 which → that

집중 훈련 2

08 who(that) painted this picture
09 who(m)(that) many children admire
10 what we saw
11 the last advice that
12 some people whose ideas
13 What the thief stole
14 the only person that passed

집중 훈련 3

15 I read the book that(which) I bought yesterday.
16 This is the very food that I ordered.
17 I do not(don't) know the man who(that) talked to me.
18 He works for a company that(which) makes shoes.
19 I have a friend whose hobby is figure skating.
20 It is the worst grade that I got this year.
21 Show me the pictures that(which) you took there.

집중 훈련 4

22 I got the email that(which) Amy sent.
23 He couldn't remember what she said.
24 I respect people who wake up early in the morning.
25 I want to know everything that you know.

01 선행사(the person)가 사람이고 관계사절에서 주어 역할을 하므로 주격 관계대명사 who(that)을 쓴다.
02 선행사(the watch)가 사물이고 관계사절에서 목적어 역할을 하므로 목적격 관계대명사 that(which)를 쓴다. 목적격 관계대명사는 생략할 수 있다.

03 선행사(the girl) 뒤에 오는 관계사절에서 관계대명사가 명사(mom) 앞에 쓰이는 소유격 역할을 하므로 소유격 관계대명사 whose를 쓴다.
04 선행사가 없으므로 선행사를 포함하는 관계대명사 what을 쓴다.
05 관계사절의 동사는 선행사(two girls)의 수에 일치시키므로 like를 쓴다.
06 선행사(a person)가 사람이고 관계사절에서 목적어 역할을 하므로 목적격 관계대명사 who(m)(that)을 쓴다. 목적격 관계대명사는 생략할 수 있다.
07 선행사(the boy and the dog)가 「사람+동물」일 때에는 관계대명사 that을 쓴다.
08 선행사(the artist)가 사람이고 관계사절에서 주어 역할을 해야 하므로 주격 관계대명사 who(that)을 쓴다.
09 선행사(astronauts)가 사람이고 관계사절에서 목적어 역할을 하므로 목적격 관계대명사 who(m)(that)을 쓴다.
10 '~하는 것'이라는 의미로 선행사를 포함하는 관계대명사 what을 쓴다.
11 선행사에 서수 표현(the last)이 있으므로 관계대명사 that을 쓴다.
12 선행사(some people) 뒤에 오는 관계사절에서 소유격 역할을 해야 하므로 명사(ideas) 앞에 소유격 관계대명사 whose를 쓴다.
13 '~하는 것'이라는 의미로 선행사를 포함하는 관계대명사 what을 쓴다.
14 선행사에 the only가 있으므로 관계대명사 that을 쓴다.
15 선행사(the book)가 사물이고 관계사절에서 목적어 역할을 해야 하므로 목적격 관계대명사 that(which)를 쓴다.
16 선행사에 the very가 있으므로 관계대명사 that을 쓴다.
17 선행사(the man)가 사람이고 관계사절에서 주어 역할을 해야 하므로 주격 관계대명사 who(that)를 쓴다.
18 선행사(a company)가 사물이고 관계사절에서 주어 역할을 해야 하므로 주격 관계대명사 that(which)를 쓴다.
19 선행사(a friend) 뒤에 오는 관계사절에서 관계대명사가 소유격 역할을 해야 하므로 명사(hobby) 앞에 소유격 관계대명사 whose를 쓴다.
20 선행사에 최상급 표현(the worst)이 있으므로 관계대명사 that을 쓴다.
21 선행사(the pictures)가 사물이고 관계사절에서 목적어 역할을 해야 하므로 목적격 관계대명사 that(which)를 쓴다.
22 선행사(the email)가 사물이고 관계사절에서 목적어 역할을 해야 하므로 목적격 관계대명사 that(which)를 쓴다.
23 '~하는 것'이라는 의미로 선행사를 포함하는 관계대명사 what을 쓴다.

24 선행사(people)가 사람이고 관계사절에서 주어 격할을 해야 하므로 주격 관계대명사 who를 쓴다.

25 선행사가 -thing으로 끝나는 대명사이므로 관계대명사 that을 쓴다.

1 the gift that(which), gave
2 Tourists who(that) like Korean dramas will visit this place.
3 Look at the house whose roof is white.
4 (1) that Kate was wearing
  (2) who was standing behind you
  (3) whose hair is long
5 (1) that is playing now at Star Cinema
  (2) what you want to see
  (3) the horror movie that Amy saw

1 선행사(the gift)가 사물이고 관계사절에서 목적어 역할을 해야 하므로 목적격 관계대명사 that(which)를 쓴다.

2 주격 관계대명사 who(that)이 이끄는 관계사절이 문장의 주어이자 선행사인 Tourists를 수식하는 형태로 쓴다.

3 선행사(the house) 뒤에 오는 관계사절에서 관계대명사가 명사(roof) 앞에 쓰이는 소유격(Its) 역할을 해야 하므로 소유격 관계대명사 whose를 사용하여 문장을 연결한다.

4 (1) 선행사에 the same이 있으므로 관계대명사 that을 쓴다.
(2) 선행사가 사람이고 관계사절에서 주어 역할을 하므로 주격 관계대명사 who를 쓴다. 선행사(The woman)에 맞춰 be동사는 was로 쓴다.
(3) 선행사(a dog) 뒤에 오는 관계사절에서 관계대명사가 명사(hair) 앞에 쓰이는 소유격 역할을 해야 하므로 관계대명사 whose를 쓴다.

5 **해석** Cindy 너 그 영화 봤니? 스타 극장에서 지금 상영 중인데.
David 아니, 아직 안 봤어. 너 그 영화 보고 싶니?
Cindy 아니. 네가 보고 싶은 것을 내게 말해 봐.
David 나는 지난 일요일에 Amy가 본 공포 영화를 보고 싶어.
→ (1) 주격 관계대명사 that이 이끄는 관계사절이 선행사인 the movie를 수식하는 형태로 쓴다.
(2) '~하는 것'이라는 의미로 선행사를 포함하는 관계대명사 what을 사용하여 쓴다.
(3) 목적격 관계대명사 that이 이끄는 관계사절이 선행사인 the horror movie를 수식하는 형태로 쓴다.

영역	브랜드	초1~2	초3~4	초5~6	중1	중2	중3	고1	고2	고3